Library Rx:
Measuring and Treating Library Anxiety
A Research Study

Martina Malvasi
Catherine Rudowsky
Jesus M. Valencia

Association of College and Re:
A division of the American Library.
Chicago, 2009

The paper used in this publication meets the minimum requirements of American National Standard for Information Sciences-Permanence of Paper for Printed Library Materials, ANSI Z39.48-1992. ∞

Library of Congress Cataloging-in-Publication Data

Malvasi, Martina.
  Library Rx : measuring and treating library anxiety, a research study / Martina Malvasi, Catherine Rudowsky, Jesus M. Valencia.
    p. cm.
  Includes bibliographical references.
  ISBN 978-0-8389-8499-4 (pbk. : alk. paper) 1. Library anxiety. 2. Libraries and students--Psychological aspects. 3. Library users--Psychology. 4. College students--Psychology. 5. Library orientation for college students--Evaluation. 6. Slippery Rock University of Pennsylvania--Case studies. I. Rudowsky, Catherine. II. Valencia, Jesus M. III. Title.
  Z718.7M35 2009
  025.501'9--dc22
                              2009005406

Printed in the United States of America.

13 12 11 10 09   5 4 3 2 1

It flies past the storm!

"We are at Grandma's house!" Olivia shouts. She gives Grandma a big hug.

Contents

Acknowledgements

We would first and foremost like to express our gratitude to Dr. Sharon Bostick. Dr. Bostick, creator of the Library Anxiety Scale, graciously granted us permission to use her scale for our research for three consecutive years. Beyond the Library Anxiety Scale, however, we are grateful for her support. Dr. Bostick demonstrated interest in our research through encouraging and enthusiastic e-mails as well as personally attending our presentation at ACRL in 2007. We are humbled by Dr. Bostick's generous spirit and are thankful to have crossed paths with her.

We would also like to thank Ms. Jane Smith, our colleague and friend. In this particular endeavor, Ms. Smith served to edit our entire manuscript during the first draft phase, spending countless hours providing meticulous comments and feedback. We are thankful to her for lending us her editing skills and an exorbitant amount of her time, but more so, we are thankful for her incredible personality and huge heart.

Next, we would like to thank the FYRST instructors from Slippery Rock University who allowed us to use their classes for our research. In 2006, the instructors were Dr. David Champion, Criminal Justice, Ms. Martina Malvasi, Library, Dr. Alison Plessinger, Communication, and Dr. David Valentine, Computer Science. In 2007, the instructors were Dr. Mark Chase, Communication, Dr. Deb Hutchins, Parks and Recreation/Environmental Education, Ms. Martina Malvasi, Library, and Dr. Bill Ryan, Exercise Science. These instructors offered valuable class time and rearranged schedules to accommodate our needs. We are grateful.

Last, but not least, we would like to thank our families. They not only tolerated us; they supported us. Martina would like to thank her three children, Nathan, Sissy, and Ben; Catherine would like to thank her husband Darren; and Jesus would like to thank his wife Amparo and his daughter Camila. Our families encouraged our research, left us in peace when we needed to work from home, and tolerated us brainstorming over dinner or while falling asleep in bed. Thank you all from each of us.

Introduction

The librarians at Slippery Rock University's (SRU) Bailey Library, not unlike other libraries across the country, found themselves frequently entangled in conversations about redesigning the reference desk, rethinking the current model of library instruction, and discovering new ways to reach out to students who are typically more comfortable asking student workers for help rather than librarians. Various scenarios, again not unique to SRU, fueled the discussions. At the same time, these scenarios were being discussed across the country at conferences, in workshops, and in consortium meetings.

One common scenario involves a student at the reference desk with a blank expression on his or her face as a librarian recites a call number. The disturbing part is not that the student does not understand the call number, but instead that the blank expression is not accompanied by a request for help. Without further assistance initiated by the librarian, such a student may simply wander aimlessly through the stacks trying to crack the codes of the Library of Congress and Melvil Dewey. Students do not ask for further assistance for many reasons, including that they think that they should know the answer, that they do not want to feel stupid, and they do not want to bother the librarian with yet another question. This fact is reinforced by students who begin their reference encounters with, "I'm sorry to bother you," followed by, "I know that I should know this, but…"

Another common encounter involves the blank expressions on the faces of the freshmen students attending library instruction sessions. These students aren't sure if it is cool to pay attention. They are more concerned with observing their classmates then becoming information literate as they work their way through social acceptance at the college level. Moreover, these students are not even sure that they need to learn what is being presented. They have no immediate need for databases and the library catalog in the first few weeks of school. Without such a context, the session has little impact. Coupling this with limited time, often fifty minutes, and hundreds of resources to demonstrate, first-semester library instruction rarely sticks with students. A month later, when they have a specific need for the information, they don't remember it and are embarrassed to ask for assistance at the reference desk.

These scenarios are portraits of library anxiety—the inadequate feeling students have when lost in overwhelming buildings that present mountains of information in all formats and professionals who may seem busy and unapproachable. Library anxiety, a grounded theory developed by Constance Mellon in 1986, explains that "when confronted with the need to gather information in the library for their research paper many students become so anxious that they are unable to approach the problem logically or effectively" (p. 163). Unfortunately, there is a great deal of evidence that library anxiety is a phenomenon experienced by a wide range of students, particularly first-year students. Further evidence indicates that the consequences of library anxiety can range from never finding a book that is on the library shelves to never completing dissertations, and thus, never finishing graduate programs.

Unfortunately, the concept of library anxiety is not new and is not going away anytime soon. Academic librarians have long been a natural source of intimidation for students. The endless rows of books coded in a foreign language, abstracts and indexes that require advanced knowledge to use, and introverted librarians who hold scholarship in high esteem have often been less than welcoming. Add an endless selection of databases, each with its own set of search rules, confusion over the difference between an electronic resource and a web resource, and an explosion of information to the mix and the stress level can only intensify. The Millennial generation, more than any generation before it, has a multitude of causes for library anxiety.

To further complicate matters, Millennials, we are told, have short attention spans, would rather communicate via technology than in person and need explicit directions. Millennials have many characteristics that do not fit well into the traditional model of classroom teaching. In response, many educators have been exploring and calling for new learning models. Libraries are not able to escape this conversation and must be ready and willing to explore new avenues of outreach to changing generations. Concepts that began as simple online tutorials have escalated into library integration with course management software, gaming in the library, and reference service offered in a multitude of ways, including instant messaging, e-mail, and texting.

In response to the scenarios and conversations revolving around library use, library anxiety, Millennials, and alternate modes of teaching, two librarians at Bailey Library at SRU with the help of an SRU economics professor skilled in statistics, determined to research solutions. The research team asked how library anxiety, particularly in first-year students who suffer the most, can be effectively reduced? Do these Millennial students experience a greater reduction in library anxiety as a result of bibliographical instruction, one-on-one instruction, online instruction, or by using the library with no intervention?

The research team believes that answering these questions is the first step on the road to information literate students. If students experience a reduction in library anxiety and learn to be comfortable using the library, they are more likely to have a healthy relationship with information. Students who view the library as an ally and a user-friendly tool in the research process will be more likely to use the library, seek help, and continually build upon their research skills. Librarians will, therefore, have more teaching moments and more opportunity to enhance student understanding of information.

1 Library Anxiety and Library Instruction: A Literature Review

General Anxiety

Arriving on campus to enter their first semester of college, many freshmen are filled with excitement and optimism. They also, however, experience significant anxiety, ranging from managing their own time to establishing new friends. Anxious situations include waking up on time for an 8:00 a.m. class, learning to navigate the campus, learning to live in a small space, establishing routines, meeting roommates and professors, making decisions, testing freedoms, maintaining a healthy and safe lifestyle, figuring out finances, and undertaking large, complex assignments. Further complicating matters, students in situations where they experience measurable anxiety responses also experience debilitating performance (Alpert 1960), and a negative impact on both social behavior and intellectual functioning (Phillips 1971).

Unfortunately many educators think that this adjustment to college life lasts only a few weeks, but according to Mary Stuart Hunter and James S. Gahagan (2003), "this process of adjustment takes place in phases that are spread over the entire first year of college." Ignoring or discounting the issues that freshmen face during their first year of college can result in tremendous costs to the institution through student attrition or poor academic performance. Colleges and universities have begun to focus on student retention; this focus has helped to create programs and initiatives that are dedicated to the first-year student. These programs and initiatives, which will be discussed in a later chapter, have begun to look at both academic and nonacademic barriers that interfere with the success of first-year college students.

As demonstrated above by Hunter and Gahagan (2003), students progress through phases in order to adjust during their first year of college. In the early fall first-year students may call home frequently, because they are feeling homesick or alone. Interactions with other students at this point may help to reduce their feelings of being emotionally overwhelmed and isolated. As the semester progresses, first-year students may begin to feel the crunch of midterms and papers. Interventions such as study groups, library instruction, or student-to-student mentoring may then help first-year students to succeed. As the fall semester draws to an end, students often feel anxious about finals, end-of-the-year projects, the holidays, or returning home. Students returning for the spring semester may once again feel homesick and anxious about starting a new semester, exacerbated by the depression often experienced from shorter winter days that force students indoors. The end of the semester also brings anxiety as students once again prepare for finals. Sadness over leaving friends and apprehension about moving back home all add dimensions to the general anxiety that most first-year students experience.

Numerous recent studies have documented that the life of modern college students are different in many ways from that of the mid-twentieth century (Hesketh 1999). As fees and tuition have steadily increased, students are experiencing greater financial burdens. In addition, with more people entering the academic world, degrees are becoming commonplace. As a result, students are faced with increasing pressures to get a good degree from a highly rated college or university. According to John Davy et. al. (2000), as higher education expands, the concern remains that the current student-support structures are not developing at an equivalent pace. "Academics, relationships, and financial difficulties have been found to be some of the major causes of stress for students" (Grant 2002) and "relationships between these variables and mental health have also been found" (Andrews and Wilding 2004; Monk 2004; Roberts and Zelenyanski 2002). In several recent studies, findings have reported, that on measures of psychological well-being, college students fare worse than the general population (Roberts and Zelenyanski 2002; Roberts et al. 1999; Stewart-Brown et al. 2000).

Realizing that students face many sources of anxiety and acknowledging that this anxiety is a detriment, it is not practical to expect a one-stop shopping answer to the problem. The sources and consequences of the anxiety are far-reaching and vastly different. It is necessary to look at individual causes of anxiety and to treat, or better yet prevent, as many sources of anxiety as possible. The purpose of this publication, therefore, is to focus on library anxiety, a well-documented source of first-year college student anxiety that, in and of itself, is complex – with varying causes, a range of consequences, and deep-rooted assumptions about resolution. "Of all forms of academic-related anxiety that prevail at the college level, library anxiety appears to be among the most common, likely because virtually every student is required to use the library at some point in their programs of study" (Onwuegbuzie and Jiao 2004, 41).

Library Anxiety

Constance Mellon, an assistant professor at East Carolina University, first described and recognized the phenomenon of library anxiety in her 1986 landmark study. Sharon Bostick later propelled this research forward developing and validating a survey instrument used to measure library anxiety. Since that time, studies have examined who experiences library anxiety, what causes library anxiety, whether or not library anxiety is connected to trait anxiety, and the consequences of library anxiety. Most of these studies have called for further research into the understanding of library anxiety, especially an attempt to identify prevention and treatment options. The knowledge that library anxiety exists and is a problem necessitates an examination of how to remedy the problem. To date few studies have focused on this aspect of the problem.

Mellon's (1986) initial goal was to study the effectiveness of library instruction; she soon realized, however, that students in her study were not discussing specific problems related to searching but rather overall feelings of fear about even beginning a search. Based on this discovery, she coined the term "library anxiety." Mellon explained that "the library phobia that they [students] described seemed to tie in loosely with the work being done on math and test anxiety. It thus seemed logical to describe students' fear in the library as library anxiety and to consider treating it within the anxiety framework" (p. 163). She also noted that 75 to 85 percent of undergraduate students described "their initial library research experiences in terms of anxiety" (p. 162). Her study concluded that anxiety stemmed from the size of the library, a lack of knowledge about locating things in the library, how to initiate library research, and how to proceed with a library search. Consequently, Mellon believed that library instruction should be approached from a broad perspective that attempts to comfort and ease students rather than teach them everything they need to know about library research. She referred to this library instruction redesign as "warmth sessions" (p. 164).

"Warmth sessions" address the negative emotions, including tension, fear, uncertainty, helplessness, self-defeat or disorganization, that students with library anxiety exhibit. These feelings and emotions reveal themselves in one or more of the six stages of the information search process (ISP): task initiation, topic selection, refocus exploration, focus formulation, information collection, or search closure (Kuhlthau 1988, 1991). Carol C. Kuhlthau (1991, 361) notes that "uncertainty and anxiety are an integral part of the [search] process, particularly in the beginning stages." Since a user's search process revolves around feelings, thoughts, and actions, the ISP involves three domains: cognitive, physical, and affective (Kuhlthau 1991). Kuhlthau believes that anxiety in the ISP is a natural occurrence and that it is in the best interests of the students that they understand the ISP and the anxiety that will most likely accompany these tasks. She believes that rather than learning how to use specific tools, students should learn about the search process.

Building upon Mellon's theory, Sharon Bostick (1992) created the Library Anxiety Scale (LAS), which is a validated and tested survey used to measure library anxiety in college students. In her own research, Bostick (1992) found that library anxiety is a multidimensional phenomenon consisting of five components:

1. barriers with staff
2. affective barriers
3. comfort with the library
4. knowledge of the library
5. mechanical barriers

Barriers with staff refers to student perceptions that librarians and staff are intimidating and aloof. Some students also perceive that librarians are too busy to help. *Affective barriers* refer to the feelings of inadequacy that students experience when trying to use the library. Students often feel that others know how to use the library and as a result feel inept, incompetent, and alone. *Comfort with the library* deals with how safe, welcome, and non-threatened students feel in the library. Students may perceive the library to be unwelcoming or even threatening and thus avoid contact with the very people who could assist them with their research. Furthermore, students can feel unsafe while wandering through dark and unpopulated stacks. *Knowledge of the library* refers to how familiar students are with using the library. *Mechanical barriers* reflects how students rely on such mechanical equipment in the library as computers, printers, copy machines, and microfilm readers. This multi-layered Library Anxiety Scale has become the standard survey for studying and understanding library anxiety.

The Library Anxious Student

Fundamental to a discussion of who the library anxious student is, is an understanding of why students use university and college libraries. Understanding why students use libraries can lead to an understanding of where anxiety resides and where intervention efforts might be focused. Qun G. Jiao and Anthony J. Onwuegbuzie in 1997 conducted a study to understand the prevalence and reasons for university library usage. They found thirteen prevailing reasons for students to use an academic library:

1. to obtain a book (74.3%);
2. to study for a test (67.1%);
3. to use the computerized indexes and online facilities (53.2%);
4. to read their own textbook (50%);
5. to study for a class project (49%);
6. to check out books (43.3%);
7. to use the photocopy machine (42.1%);
8. to read reserve materials (38.9%);
9. to search and obtain information for a thesis/dissertation (36.4%);
10. to return a book (32%);
11. to read current newspapers (31.8%);
12. to meet friends (31.4%);
13. to find out information about potential employers (28.4%).

Jiao and Onwuegbuzie also found that the frequency of library visits did not vary according to the year in school; the reason, however, for visiting the library did. Older students were more likely to visit the library to do research and read current newspapers. Other findings included that non-English speaking students visit the library more frequently than their native counterparts, and that males visit the library more to study for a test or meet with friends while females visit the library more to obtain a book or article. Understanding how and why students do or don't use academic libraries may lead to a better understanding of the areas in which anxiety resides.

To further aid in this understanding, numerous studies have explored the concept of library anxiety. Many of these studies advanced library anxiety research by focusing on understanding the library anxious student and exactly who suffers from this anxiety. By doing so, library services and library instruction can be tailored to best handle highly anxious library users. Jiao and Onwuegbuzie have conducted several of these studies and have reported relationships between library anxiety and personal characteristics. In a series of studies conducted by Jiao et. al (1996), the authors found that students with high levels of library anxiety were young, male, spoke English as a second language, had high levels of academic achievement, held a job, and visited the library infrequently. The strongest correlation was discovered between level of anxiety and frequency of library visits; those students with the highest levels of anxiety tend to use the library the least often. Furthermore, this study found levels of anxiety to be higher in freshmen and sophomores than any other level, with freshmen having the highest levels.

In 1998, Onwuegbuzi and Jiao concluded that library anxious students tend to be those students who like structure, are self-motivated, who lack persistence, and who are peer-oriented learners. In addition, library anxious students do not like to undertake difficult tasks in the afternoon and require mobility in learning environments. Some students with certain characteristics are more vulnerable to specific library anxieties. Perfectionists, for example tend to have higher levels of library anxiety associated with affective and mechanical barriers and comfort with the library. "Students who have the poorest sense of successful determination in relation to their goals, and who have the least positive appraisals of their ability to generate ways to overcome goal-related obstacles have the highest level of library anxiety associated with comfort with the library and knowledge of the library" (Jiao and Onwuegbuzie 1999c, 279). Further studies by Onwuegbuzie and Jiao found that students who perceive themselves to have low levels of academic self-competence, intellectual ability, creativity, and social competence tend to have the highest levels of library anxiety associated with affective barriers and comfort with the library (Jiao and Onwuegbuzie 1999a, 145).

In 1999 Jiao and Onwuegbuzie designed a study that identifies the relationship between learning modality preferences and library anxiety. "Learning modalities pertain to the manner in which individuals typically acquire, retain, and retrieve information" (Felder and Henriques 1995). Most experts believe that individuals are born with specific tendencies toward particular learning modalities that determine how that person typically reacts to and utilizes stimuli in learning (Cornett 1983). In order to identify any potential relationships, Jiao and Onwuegbuzie used canonical correlation analysis, "a statistical technique that breaks down the association between two sets of variables and is appropriate for describing the number and nature of mutually independent relationships between the sets" (1999a, 142). The purpose of their research project was to identify the relationship between learning modalities and how this relationship could explain the debilitative effects of library anxiety. Twenty learning modalities were correlated with Bostick's five library anxiety dimensions[1]:

1. "Barriers with staff" correlated significantly with persistence, visual, and mobility.
2. "Affective barriers" related significantly to structure, visual, tactile, evening, afternoon, and mobility.
3. "Comfort with the library" associated significantly with persistence, responsibility, structure, tactile, kinesthetic, and mobility.
4. "Knowledge of the library" correlated significantly to persistence, responsibility, and mobility.
5. "Mechanical barriers" was related significantly to noise, persistence, responsibility, and mobility (Jiao and Onwuegbuzie 1999a, 208).

Students, therefore, whose perception of librarians serves to heighten their anxiety tend to be less persistent, like to receive information visually, and require mobility in learning environments. Students for whom affective barriers increase library anxiety tend to prefer structure, to receive information visually, not to process information tactilely, and to undertake difficult tasks in the morning but not in the evening. Students who do not perceive the library to be safe, welcoming, and non-threatening tend to be less persistent and responsible and to prefer structure and mobility in their learning environment. They also do not want to receive information via the tactile and kinetic modes. Students whose lack of knowledge about the library increases their anxiety tended

---

1.   The twenty learning modalities included noise, light, temperature, design, motivation, persistence, responsibility, structure, peer orientation, authority orientation, multiple perception, auditory, visual, tactile, kinesthetic, intake, evening, morning, afternoon, and mobility.

to be less persistent, responsible, and require mobility in the learning environment. Finally, students for whom mechanical library equipment increases library anxiety tend to be less persistent and responsible, prefer to work while surrounded by noise, and require mobility in learning environments. Furthermore, the canonical correlations also suggest that students who prefer to work in a quiet environment, like structure, prefer to undertake difficult tasks in the morning and prefer not to receive information tactilely tend to have higher levels of library anxiety associated with affective barriers, comfort with the library, and mechanical barriers. However, students who prefer to work surrounded by noise and require mobility in learning environments have higher levels of library anxiety associated with barriers with staff, affective barriers, knowledge of the library, and mechanical barriers.

Jiao and Onwuegbuzie continued their research in 2002, when they studied the relationship between library anxiety and social interdependence, which is shaped by cooperative, competitive, and individualistic attitudes. Jiao and Onwuegbuzie discovered a social context to library anxiety—that students with cooperative attitudes have the lowest level of anxiety with barriers with staff, comfort with the library, and knowledge of the library. This then attributed to the fact that students with a cooperative orientation are more likely to seek out help and support from others (p. 76). Conversely, individualistic students have the least anxiety with affective barriers and mechanical barriers.

Library anxiety studies have also been conducted to test for a correlation between library anxiety and trait anxiety, which defines reactions to stressful situations (Spielberger 1972). Trait anxiety is a permanent and consistent personality characteristic, unlike state anxiety, which is situation specific (Phillips 1971). Trait anxiety produces an anxious person while state anxiety produces anxious situations. Studies have questioned if those students who experience library anxiety are anxious by nature and suffer from trait anxiety or if library anxiety is a separate, situation specific phenomenon that is characteristic of state anxiety.

Terrence Mech and Charles Brooks (1995, 1997) studied library anxiety as manifested in undergraduate students. Specifically, their research tested for correlations between library anxiety and trait anxiety as well as differences or similarities in anxiety scores across college school years. In their 1995 study, Mech and Brooks reported no difference in trait anxiety among freshmen, sophomores, juniors, and seniors.

Freshmen, however, had significantly higher scores of library anxiety as compared to sophomores, juniors, and seniors. Furthermore, their research led them to conclude that library anxiety is different from a general tendency to be anxious; students who suffer from library anxiety do not necessarily suffer from trait anxiety. Library anxiety is caused by the library and related assignments not a personality characteristic. Mech and Brooks continued their research and, in 1997, reported that trait anxiety scores correlated with academic measures, including Scholastic Aptitude Test scores, high school academic rank, and first-semester college grade-point average. On the other hand, library anxiety scores did not have a correlation with these academic measures. Library anxiety, therefore, is not related to academic ability. Both studies, then, found that library anxiety is specific to the library environment and is unrelated to trait anxiety, leading the authors to posit that early intervention that acknowledges the existence and legitimacy of the anxiety would be a better approach, rather than teaching sophisticated information skills.

Jiao and Onwuegbuzie (1999c) compared library anxiety and trait anxiety when questioning the importance of library anxiety. While Mech and Brooks examined undergraduate students, Jiao and Onwuegbuzie focused on graduate students. Their findings, however, substantiated those of Mech and Brooks, when they reported that library anxiety is not a result of trait anxiety and represents its own phenomenon. They further concluded that, given the evidence that library anxiety is situation-specific, "researchers and practitioners alike should turn their attention to the treatment and reduction of library anxiety" (1999c, 281).

Causes/Dimensions of Library Anxiety

Constance Mellon (1986), who first noted the impact of library anxiety, attribute it to four causes: the size of the library, a lack of knowledge about where things are located, how and where to begin research, and the role the library plays in the research process. Mellon commented on the overwhelmingly inadequate feelings students have when first approaching an academic library. These feelings fester and build the anxiety to increased heights.

In 1991, Judith Andrews studied students' library use problems. Her research consisted of a series of interviews with students to pinpoint specific areas of difficulty related to using the library. Her goal was to correct these problems and make the library easier and more comfortable to use. Andrews found a wide range of problems including "problems with the catalogue, with locating books, the classification scheme and library layout" (Andrews 1991, 7). Other problems reported by students included a perceived lack of information about library services, feelings of being overwhelmed, and a reluctance to ask for help. Andrews reported that students prefer to ask friends and peers for help rather than a librarian, partly because they feel inadequacy. All of these problems, rooted in confusion and feelings of ignorance, lead to anxiety when faced with using the library.

The five dimensions Sharon Bostick outlined in the Library Anxiety Scale, barriers with staff, affective barriers, comfort with the library, knowledge of the library, and mechanical barriers, further explains why students are anxious when visiting the library. Everything from the perceived helpfulness of the librarians and the library staff to the photocopiers can heighten student stress. Bostick found that while some students suffer anxiety related to each of the dimensions, some students suffer anxiety related to only a few of the dimensions.

In 1993 Jane Keefer cited "library noise" or such aspects of place, as call numbers, stacks, rows, aisles, signs, maps, periodical sections, computer systems, abstracts and indexes, microfilms, and fiche as overwhelming amplifiers of anxiety about assignments, especially early in the research process. Keefer points out that literally hundreds of details can derail a student. As students continue their research and slowly learn the details, time limitations and deadlines regenerate anxiety. Keefer relates this stress to classical conditioning theory where the phenomenon is termed overdrive. Much like the hungry rats in Bruner's classic experiments, the students experience a need in a more than normal or average manner, and the intense need degrades or limits their cognitive abilities rattling them and making them less capable of thinking through situations.

In their 1997 study to determine the reasons for library use, Jiao and Onwuegbuzi found that students who visit the library to use online facilities and computerized indexes have the highest level of anxiety. This is consistent with Bostick's findings in which she reported that mechanical barriers are a major component of library anxiety. Numerous studies, in fact, demonstrate a clear link between library anxiety and technology.

According to Jiao and Onwuegbuzie (2004), rapid technological changes in the development of digital information networks and electronic services have expanded both the role of the academic library as well as the existence of library anxiety. Libraries today are vastly different from libraries of yesterday. Materials are available via many venues in many formats and students must learn how to navigate each possible pathway. The delivery of information where and when it is needed is now possible because of these technological advances. These changes have provided students with sophisticated library searching options. At the same time, however, options have undoubtedly created a new kind of anxiety. Jiao and Onwuegbuzie note that "the new technologies and electronic databases have led to students experiencing other forms of negative states" and that "it is likely that library anxiety experienced by students is, in part, a function of their attitudes toward computers" (p. 138). In 2004 Jiao and Onwuegbuzie's studied ninety-four African American graduate students enrolled at a historically black college in the eastern U.S. They concluded that "students' computer attitudes impact their willingness to engage in computer-related activities in colleges and universities where effectively using library electronic resources represents an increasingly important part of education. Negative computer attitudes may inhibit students' interests in learning to use the library resources and thereby weaken academic performances while elevating library anxiety" (Jiao and Onwuegbuzie 2004, 139).

Karen Antell's research in 2004 focused on why college students who have access to an academic library choose to use public libraries instead. After interviewing seventeen students, most of whom where non-traditional, she noted five distinct categories among their responses: personal convenience, materials, ease of use and familiarity, staff, and subjective appeal. Among those factors she included in personal convenience were family-friendliness and the convenience of location and parking. Materials included the usefulness, availability, and variety of materials in the collection. Besides the obvious definitions associated with ease of use and familiarity, she also included in that category the manageable size of many public libraries. Subjective appeal focused on the atmosphere in the facilities. The staff category included such factors as the relative friendliness and helpfulness of the staff at public libraries as opposed to those in their academic counterparts. The responses in the staff category were especially striking in their unanimity. All seventeen students found public librarians to be more approachable, friendly, and helpful. They praised public librarians for personally showing them to materials in the stacks in contrast to academic librarians who tended to simply explain where to find an item. They also had difficulty differentiating the reference desk from the circulation desk in academic libraries. The respondents did not understand the organizational structure of academic libraries, often lumping staff and student workers in with librarians. Many of Antell's finding served to reinforce those of Mellon—even twenty years later.

Consequences of Library Anxiety

The level of library anxiety a student experiences falls on a continuum that ranges from low anxiety to high anxiety. "Library-anxious students experience more interfering responses during various stages of the information search process and, as such, tend to focus less of their energy and attention on the task itself, thus impeding their learning process" (Jiao and Onwuegbuzie 1997, 373). For the high anxiety student, the library becomes the enemy and library experiences are negative. These high-anxiety students, once forced to enter the library will have difficulty navigating their way. They often miss or overlook directional signs and cues, refrain from asking for help, or simply give up all too quickly and make their exit (Jiao and Onwuegbuzie 1997; Keefer 1993). Once freed from the confines of the library these students tend to conceal their anxiety out of shame, embarrassment, or feeling inept (Jiao and Onwuegbuzie 1997; Keefer 1993). Thereafter, they do their best to avoid the library all together. This avoidance behavior prevents the high-anxiety student from developing appropriate information literacy skills.

Jiao and Onwuegbuzie argue that these students "who are anxious about seeking help from a librarian tend to produce research proposals of lower quality" (1999b, 204). Jiao and Onwuegbuzie also hypothesize that library anxiety and the avoidance behavior that it promotes lead to graduate students not completing theses and dissertations, which promotes failure in their graduate programs. Consequences of library anxiety, then, can range from poor academic papers to a complete failure to complete programs and earn degrees.

Estimations of procrastination among college students indicate that almost 95 percent put off academic tasks, including writing research papers, keeping up with weekly readings or studying for exams (Onwuegbuzie and Jiao 2000, 45). Academic procrastination has been associated with "missing deadlines for submitting assignments, delaying the taking of self-paced quizzes, claiming test anxiety, receiving low course grades, and attaining low cumulative grade point averages" (Onwuegbuzie and Jiao 2000, 45). A correlate of this estimate is that students often procrastinate about going to the library to do research. In a 2000 study, Onwuegbuzie and Jiao found a relationship between academic procrastination and library anxiety, specifically the dimensions of affective barriers, comfort with the library, and mechanical barriers. Furthermore, they found that academic procrastination that results from fear of failure and task aversion relates to the dimensions of barriers with staff, affective barriers, comfort with the library, and knowledge of the library. It is unclear whether academic procrastination causes library anxiety or whether library anxiety promotes academic procrastination, but Onwuegbuzie and Jiao believe it to be a bi-directional relationship with a cycle that is likely to continue until levels of both are maximized.

In 2004, Onwuegbuzie and Jiao applied Wine's Cognitive-Attentional-Interference theory to the library context. This theory argues that while individuals are processing information their level of anxiety drives cognitive interference, which is characterized by a shift in focus form task-relevant to task-irrelevant thoughts and actions. Onwuegbuzie and Jiao argued that "Wine's theory predicts that library anxiety hinders information search performance by impeding students' ability to receive, to concentrate on, and to encode information necessary for the research proposal" (p. 50). They explain that library anxiety decreases memory processes and relates to cognitive interference, in which a student shifts from task-relevant to task-irrelevant thoughts, making it difficult to adequately review literature and promoting avoidance behaviors (p. 50).

Intervention for Library Anxiety

In study after study, library anxiety is demonstrated as a cause of procrastination and avoidance behavior, which in turn leads to poor academic performance. The consequences of library anxiety are clear and detrimental, ranging from nervous patrons fumbling through the library to poor academic performance to failing to graduate from a program. Given this understanding, it is vital that library professionals take measures to adequately and completely address library anxiety. Some of the studies discussed above, do in fact, call for further research into the treatment and reduction of library anxiety (Jiao and Onwuegbuzie 1997, 1999a). Almost all of them devote some space to hypothesizing about possible treatments and intervention, including recognizing the anxiety, and assuring students, both that feelings of anxiety are normal and that librarians are there to help.

Mellon (1986) reports that the librarians at her university had long realized that a fifty-minute library session was not sufficient time to develop a true understanding of the search process or appropriate research tools; however, prior to her research, they did not recognize how important it was for students to simply understand that the librarians want to help them. She spearheaded a dramatic change in library instruction sessions, redesigning them as "warmth sessions." While search strategies and tools were still emphasized, the sessions prompted interaction between the students and the librarian and spent time explaining library anxiety and the fact that it is a common and reasonable feeling.

Miriam E. Joseph (1991), Jane Keefer (1993), and Lynn Westbrook and Sharon DeDecker (1993) all support the notion that before students can learn research skills, they must become comfortable with the library and the librarians. Joseph, who believes that attitude enhance the ability to learn, bluntly explains that she has less concern for the library skills of first-year students than she does for developing a positive attitude. Students must see librarians as friends rather than foes and as educators rather than hall monitors. Keefer (1993) states that she has "come to believe that a part of what we do at the reference desk in academic libraries must include helping students understand the normality of their frustration with the system. Lectures and instruction programs that let students know that everybody experiences anxiety and that asking for help is an important part of the search process can go a long way toward making students' initial library experiences less stressful." (p. 337). Westbrook (1993) believes that the normal principals of service make the assumption that students are "sufficiently comfortable and welcome in the library to approach the staff and take advantage of their services" (p. 44). She points out, however, that most librarians know that this is not true, at least to some extent. Westbrook then cites several studies that examine interpersonal means of encouraging users to request assistance, and points out that there are many ways in which librarians can step back from this historical assumption and encourage library patrons to have a level of comfort in the library and with the librarians.

Mech and Brooks (1995) believe that their research findings show a clear need for early intervention, particularly among freshmen and sophomores. The authors believe that students should be given an honest introduction into the realistic complications of library research and should be reassured that the confusion and uneasiness that they feel is a natural part of the search process and is experienced by all students. Along with skill development, students need to learn confidence in their abilities to perform library research.

Jiao, Onwuegbuzie, and Art A. Lichtenstein (1996) suggest that a one-time library instruction session is not the answer, but that library instruction should be woven holistically throughout a class and integrated in assignments. Faculty, in turn, should assist their students as they begin library research, when anxiety is often at its highest, and should accompany their students to the library where they can act as a liaison between the students and the librarians. Throughout the process, students should be made aware of the research process and taught to understand the complexities of library research so that they have more successful library experiences.

Despite the calls for further research and the anecdotal discussion about easing library anxiety, little research has been done to test various interventions and treatments that actively and accurately reduce library anxiety. One such study was carried out in 2003 by Anna Van Scoyoc. Van Scoyoc tested to see whether computer-assisted instruction (CAI) or bibliographic instruction (BI) were more or less effective at reducing library anxiety in first-year students when compared to one another and to a control group. CAI is defined by Alan Salisbury as "a man-machine interaction in which the teaching function is accomplished by a computer system without intervention by a human instructor" (Salisbury 1971, 48). BI is traditional training in library use. Van Scoyoc's research used Bostick's Library Anxiety Scale, administering it as a pre-test and post-test one week apart. The interventional instruction took place during the intermediate week. Van Scoyoc's study found that "students who took part in bibliographic instruction led by a library staff member experienced significantly less overall library anxiety compared to the control group. The same could not be said for students completing the computer-based tutorial" (Van Scoyoc 2003, 329). In addition to her overall findings, Van Scoyoc reported on two specific library anxiety dimensions, barriers with staff and affective barriers. In the case of barriers with staff, the BI session led to reduced anxiety; neither the control group, however, nor the group who used CAI succeeded in easing library anxiety. On the other hand, with affective barriers, both BI and CAI led to reduced anxiety, and only the control group was unsuccessful in experiencing reduced anxiety.

Library Instruction

Fundamental to the discussion of library anxiety is library instruction. In the case of library anxiety, as in other stresses, intervention is indicated. Most often that intervention has occurred either in formalized settings, either classroom instruction or CAI, or in informal reference desk encounters, one-on-one teaching moments. With increasingly available e-resources, a generation of students sometimes known as the "Net Generation," and expanding distance education programs, it is no wonder that the discussion of classroom instruction versus computer-assisted instruction looms large.

Library instruction is not a new concept. Academic library instruction can be traced as far back as Germany in the seventeenth century (Lorenzen 2001); some believe it is even older. The origins of library education in the United States can be traced back over 185 years to 1820, when a librarian lectured to undergraduates at Harvard College (Tiefel 1995). Library instruction in the United States is more easily traced to the late nineteenth century, when academic librarians began teaching in the classroom and writing about it (Lorenzen 2001). At least seventeen institutions of higher education adopted library instruction lectures or courses in the nineteenth century, but by 1900, six of the seventeen had withdrawn these offerings (Tiefel 1995). Throughout the late nineteenth and early twentieth centuries, library instruction experienced a roller-coaster ride. Various academic institutions regularly adopted and then dropped it from the curriculum. Between 1876 and 1932 the focus of library education moved from using materials for research to instruction on accessing materials (Tiefel 1995). Teaching basic skills to first-year students began in 1907 and was criticized as shallow starting in the late 1920s (Tiefel 1995).

While library instruction and the debate surrounding it continued throughout the first half of the twentieth century, it did not become standard until the 1960s (Lorenzen 2001; Tiefel 1995). Two changes fueled this reemergence (Hopkins, 1982). First, the development of academic specialization, and second, a new complexity in libraries that were now geared toward not only undergraduate students, but faculty and graduate students. In light of these trends, instruction began to focus on access skills and bibliographic tools (Tiefel 1995).

Library instruction continues to evolve and raise debate. Currently, library user education often focuses on the many sources of information available rather than the mechanics of using any one resource or the library system (Tiefel 1995). Many instruction librarians also focus on search strategies, which teach students research techniques. Librarians have also embraced information literacy standards, which include the need to teach critical-thinking skills that enable students to evaluate and select the best information resources for their needs.

Teaching in the library has always been and continues to be a source of debate. While many strong proponents have advocated for librarians as teachers, equally strong opposition exists to this concept. The opposition has primarily focused on three criticisms (Young 1980):

1. Library instruction is not part of the mission of providing information to patrons;
2. Library education does not work to educate library patrons;
3. Librarians do not fit well in the academic model of classroom teacher.

Anita R. Schiller in 1965, Mary Biggs in 1979, and N.M. Davidson in 1983 all focused on the first criticism, believing that teaching in the library detracted from information-providing responsibilities, both in the form of time and money. The main role of the library, each asserted, is to provide information (Lorenzen 2001). Time used to provide instruction was time not devoted to providing information.

The second criticism questions the effectiveness of library instruction. Shrigley in 1981 believed that there was a tendency for librarians to go into "overkill" mode and present too much information during a library instruction class (Lorenzen 2001). Because this information was too much for students to absorb, she proposed that one-on-one targeted instruction was more effective. Tom Eadie, one of the foremost critics of library instruction, originally favored instruction. In 1990, however, he argued that it was largely a waste of time, as librarians were trying to teach students how to answer questions that had not yet been asked (Lorenzen 2001). Like Shrigley, he believed that one-on-one, point-of-need assistance at the reference desk was more effective and a better use of time. Frances L. Hopkins (1982) argued against these critics, asserting that library instruction is not intended to make students independent, but has purposes instead to make them confident and comfortable with using the reference desk and asking questions. Hopkins arguments could be viewed as advocating library instruction as a means of reducing library anxiety.

The final critique of library instruction is that librarians do not fit into the academic model of classroom teacher; suggesting that librarians use instruction to justify their status as faculty and to improve their status on campus (Lorenzen 1995). It is sometimes believed that library instruction is counter-productive, and in 1979, Patrick Wilson argued that academic librarians imagine that faculty have greater status as a result of teaching. Librarians, therefore, create ways to teach. As with the other criticisms, however, there are countless counter-arguments; most simply to dismiss the claim that library instruction has self-perpetuating motives. Hopkins (1981) again argued against the critics of library instruction by addressing this last criticism. She argued that the relationship between faculty and libraries is neither helped nor hindered by librarians as teachers and that it did not impact status on campus. If it does not impact status, than this cannot be a motive for teaching, countering the final criticism.

Today, the debate surrounding library instruction often involves the mode of delivery. As with all education, the presence of increased technology, tech-savvy students, and distance education programs have opened avenues for delivery methods. Historically debate has focused on whether classroom instruction or one-on-one assistance at the reference desk serve to be more effective in educating library users. In recent decades, the use of computer-assisted instruction (CAI) has entered the debate.

CAI was first used in libraries as early as 1970s, beginning with the University of Denver, the University of Illinois at Urbana, and the Ohio State University (Holman 2000). Many library educators will argue that with online resources gaining in prevalence over traditional resources and with today's tech-savvy student population, hands-on, active learning via technology is the best route for delivering library instruction. This discussion, however, most often revolves around teaching specific skills.

In 2000 Lucy Holman conducted a study at the University of North Carolina to determine whether students perform skills, such as using the online catalog and locating reserve materials, better after completing a CAI program or after participating in a classroom session. Holman's discussion focused on teaching practical skills and points out that previous studies, from 1988 and 1989, found CAI to be more effective in teaching specific skills to undergraduates. Holman, however, found that while both the CAI and the classroom instruction group showed improvements over the control group, no significant difference was apparent between the CAI and classroom instruction groups (Holman 2000). Holman concludes that "it would appear that if both instruction methods work equally well with students, each institution can make instruction decisions based on its staff and space" (2000, 58).

Li Zhang, Erin M. Watson, and Laura Banfield (2007) conducted a study comparing the efficacy of face-to-face instruction with CAI in the library. They first outline the most frequently cited advantages and disadvantages of CAI, explaining that on one hand, students can work at their own pace, it provides increased accessibility, and saves librarians time. On the other hand, CAI programs are expensive and labor intensive to develop, do not provide personal interactions between students and librarians, and make it difficult for students to ask questions and get immediate feedback. The authors also cite numerous prior studies testing the effectiveness of CAI compared to face-to-face instruction in academic libraries and point out that these studies have mixed results, some finding each method to be equally effective and others finding a clear winner. In their study, they found CAI and face-to-face instruction to be equally effective for delivering basic library skills.

Summary

There is clear evidence in the literature that library anxiety is a real and threatening phenomena that affects students negatively. There has been ample research on the causes and consequences of library anxiety. Realizing these causes and wanting to circumvent the consequences, it is imperative that academic libraries take measures to treat and reduce library anxiety. It is most obvious for this intervention to be a form of instruction, be it one-on-one at the reference desk, classroom instruction, or CAI. Librarians as teachers, however, as well as the effectiveness of library instruction have long been debated. There is a need, therefore, for a study to thoroughly and accurately look at various treatment methods as compared to no treatment to determine which has the greatest probability of reducing library anxiety, especially in first-year students—who suffer the most anxiety.

2 The Millennial Generation

Although the authors of this book are neither sociologists nor anthropologists, we do teach students who are part of the Millennial generation. We recognize, both from experience and observation, the differences among the needs and wants of the Millennials and those of Gen-Xer's and Baby Boomers. In order to report accurate research about the Millennial generation, the authors will be relying on well-cited experts, including Neil Howe and William Strauss as well as numerous other published works.

Generation Categories

Generations spanning the twentieth and twenty-first century are generally broken down into five categories: GI generation (1901-1924), Silent generation (1924-1942), Baby Boom generation (1943-1960), Generation X (1961-1981), and Millennial generation (1982-2002) (Howe and Strauss 2000). These generations have different values and priorities. The GI and Silent generations, for example, respect authority, embrace family, and value community involvement. Boomers are optimistic workaholics who possess strong work ethics. Gen-Xers are skeptical multi-taskers who dislike red tape and seek a work-family balance. Millennials are hopeful, appreciate technology and are close with their parents; they scorn anything that is slow or reflects negativity. In order to effectively communicate with and teach each one of these generations, it is necessary to understand them.

The Millennials

What are the core tendencies of these Millennial generation college students? According to Howe and Strauss (2000), their primary traits are:
- Special
- Sheltered
- Confident
- Conventional
- Team oriented
- Achievers
- Pressured

These traits, in most cases, have been shaped by outside forces, especially authority figures—primarily parents.

Parents of Millennials have repeatedly told their children that they are special. "They have been made to feel vital to their parent's sense of purpose" (DeBard 2004, 35). In fact, according to Shapiro (2002, 23), "one of the ancillary aspects of serving Millennial students is dealing constructively with their intrusive parents." Children in the Millennial generation, for example, were awarded with trophies for participation rather than for victory. They were made to feel important and valued, simply for showing-up. Strauss and Howe (1991) have described the Millennials as the "civic" generation. The Millennials perceive coming-of-age as "good" and "empowering", whereas Generation X perceived it as "bad" and "alienating" (p. 365).

Millennial children have been sheltered from birth. "Baby on board" signs in minivans, photo ID kits, and safety rules demonstrate how well this generation has been protected. Encouraged to follow rules and regulations, the Millennials have come to expect clearly communicated rules that will be enforced with due process (Martin and Tulgan 2001). Millennial parents have succeeded at structuring the lives of their children. They participated in after-school programs, played on soccer leagues or belonged to the traveling hockey team, studied music, karate, and dance and had scheduled play dates. Free playtime has been rescheduled (Howe and Strauss 2000). Millennial parents sheltered their children by mandating this rigorous schedule in an effort to provide some sort of supervision for their children at all times. As a result, the Millennial generation has come to trust and count on authority figures.

Often referred to as the ambitious generation, Schneider and Stevenson (1999) have found that Millennial children indeed have high ambitions but lack clear direction. Despite their lack of direction though, they are confident, one of the other documented traits of Millennials. When liberated in college, though, the lack of direction exceeds their confidence and they often seem aimless. Because of the superimposed nature of the goals they grew up with, Millennial students are underprepared to assume direction in their lives. Unfortunately, these children were not afforded any opportunities, during their formative years, to create their own schedules or to direct their lives. As a result, when they enter college and are placed into an environment that requires self-direction, the Millennials become lost.

Howe and Strauss (2000) have described the Millennial student as highly conventional. They accept the social rules that their Boomer parents have defined and imposed upon them. They have learned that the best way to get along is to go along (Sax 2003), thus reinforcing their lack of purpose.

Millennial students are drawn to teams and they enjoy a team-oriented approach. Howe and Strauss (2000) have suggested that Millennials want to be perceived as cooperative by those in positions to judge. They are upbeat about working with others on projects, perhaps because teamwork lowers the pressure on the individual. For them, collective action is viewed as a positive environment. Although Millennial students embrace the team-oriented approach, they also want their projects to be highly structured (Howe and Strauss 2000). They need their Boomer mentors to ensure that project goals are achievable.

Millennial generation members strongly crave such achievement (DeBard 2004). They are more likely to accept accountability if that accountability can be achieved through good behavior (DeBard 2004). In fact, they closely link behavior and achievement. They expect, for example, high grades as a reward for compliance to academic standards. If a Millennial student has perfect attendance in class and other behaviors that comply with academic standards, he or she will expect a high grade. They expect to be rewarded for their participation not their performance. Like the soccer trophy rewarded to them as children, these students also expect to be rewarded with high grades in college.

According to a study sponsored by The Cooperative Institutional Research Program (CIRP), academic standards in high schools are lax (Sax 2003). Among today's high school students, 45.7 percent earn an "A" average; in 1968 only 17.6 percent were "A" students. It seems that the system has responded to the participation model for rewards; academic standards allow more students to be validated with good grades. Millennial students anticipate high grades but are only willing to do the minimum expected of them to achieve their desired outcomes (Sax 2003). This clearly presents a challenge to educators working with Millennial students.

Finally, Millennial students feel pressured, the last of the seven traits outlined by Howe and Strauss. As children, their Baby Boomer parents pushed them to achieve, created opportunities for them to achieve, and rewarded them for good behavior. As a result, Millennial students feel pressured to perform and excel in order to meet their parents' and society's expectations. These same Millennial students, however, have come to rely on their parents for structure and a well-organized path to success (Howe and Strauss 2000). When parents continue to meet their needs, this relieves some of the pressure. It also, unfortunately, reduces their need to improvise or be creative.

Millennials have been encouraged to believe in themselves and to feel special. While being sheltered and structured, they have been taught to be confident and to trust in their future. As a result, they are conventional by nature. Their sometimes over-structured lives have also led to a strong reliance on group activities and team-oriented approaches. They have been rewarded for agreeing to participate in activities. They are motivated to meet their own expectations as well as the expectations of others, as long as there are beneficial outcomes. In essence, achievement for them is about tangible rewards. As a result of the special treatment, the structure, and the idea of constant rewards for achievement, this generation often feels pressure, which is alleviated by looking to past generations for direction.

In order to fully appreciate the differences between generations, Howe and Strauss (2000) designed a table that compares the responses of each generation to twelve descriptors.

As outlined in Table 2.1, some differences exist among generational responses. Understanding these differences can enable educators to better serve the current Millennial generation. Teaching methods, communication styles, and teacher-student relationships can be modeled to meet their specific views.

Millennials & Technology

The Millennial generation has been raised with computers; being connected, for them, is as important as the air they breathe. The technology available to each generation influences not only their behaviors, including how they learn and how they communicate, but also their expectations. The Silent Generation (1924 – 1942), for example, grew up using vacuum-tube radios, mechanical calculators, 78-rpm records, and dial telephones; Boomers (1943-1960) had transistor radios, mainframe computers, 33- and 45-rpm records, and touch tone telephones. Generation X enjoyed CDs, personal computers, and e-mail. The Millennials, on the other hand, have enjoyed a

Table 2.1. Generational Differences

Views Toward	Generations		
	Boomers	Gen Xers	Millennials
Levels of trust	Confident of self, not authority	Low toward authority	High toward authority
Loyalty to institutions	Cynical	Considered naïve	Committed
Most admire	Taking charge	Creating enterprise	Following a hero of integrity
Career goals	Build a stellar career	Build a portable career	Build parallel careers
Rewards	Title and the corner office	Freedom not to do	Meaningful work
Parent-Child Involvement	Receding	Distant	Intruding
Having Children	Controlled	Doubtful	Definite
Family Life	Indulged as children	Alienated as children	Protected as children
Education	Freedom of expression	Pragmatic	Structure of accountability
Evaluation	Once a year with documentation	"Sorry, but how am I doing?"	Feedback whenever I want it
Political Orientation	Attack oppression	Apathetic, individual	Crave community
The Big Question	What does it mean?	Does it work?	How do we build it?

complex, technology rich environment of cell phones, MP3 and MP4 players, PDAs, IM, text messaging, and blogs (Hartman, Moskal, and Dziuban 2005). They have played video games, downloaded music, used Facebook and MySpace, watched podcasts, and IMed or texted with friends. They are not so much aware of the technology behind their activities as the activities themselves (Oblinger and Oblinger 2005). As a result, they are not avid readers, hate busywork, learn better by doing, and want instant feedback and gratification (*How the New Generation* 2007).

This plethora of technology has led the Millennial generation to develop a different learning and communication style from their predecessors. Millennials, for example, are visual learners; they prefer visual learning to text. Because of the number of video games that they play, they possess strong visual-spatial skills, which help them integrate the virtual and the physical. This generation also learns better through discovery than through lecture. They are much better than other generations at shifting their attention rapidly from one task to another; however, they often choose not to pay attention to things that do not interest them. Millennials respond quickly and expect a quick response in return. They want instant gratification in everything that they do (Oblinger and Oblinger 2005). In addition, Millennials do not process information in the same way as previous generations. According to Marc Prensky (2001, 3), Millennials have "developed hypertext minds, they leap around," thus linear thinking is not common. Also, they do not possess a strong ability to synthesize information from different sources (Oblinger and Oblinger 2005).

Although the Millennials are comfortable being surrounded by and using technology to both learn and communicate, this does not mean that they are digitally literate. In fact, most do not have an understanding of technology or possess the abilities to judge the quality of their resources (Oblinger and Oblinger 2005). In a survey conducted in 2002 by Steve Jones, 73 percent of the students surveyed stated that they are more likely to use the Internet for research than go to the library (p. 3). Two-thirds of students also affirmed that they knew how to find valid information on the Web (Online Computer Library Center 2002, 2). Based on years of observations and experience, educators know that this is not the case. Students are not information-literate; most take the first five hits from a Google search and use that information as the basis for projects.

Educating the Millennials

How then can librarians and educators meet the educational needs of these technology-connected Millennial students? What changes in teaching need to be made in order to accommodate their learning style? How much change is needed? What about the next generation; will these changes work for them? How can we meet the needs of a generation that prefers to learn by doing, requires structure, wants interactivity, enjoys group work, refuses to read large amounts of text, and often refuses to pay attention in class if it is too slow, is unengaging, or is simply uninteresting (Prensky 2001)?

Opportunities and challenges exist within the Millennials' blended behaviors and attitudes, from their familiarity with technology, multitasking accomplishments, and team- work orientation, to their acceptance of authority and diversity (Hartman, Moskal, and Dziuban 2005). The challenges with Millennials arise from their "comparative lack of critical thinking skills, naïve views on intellectual property and the authenticity of information found on the Internet" (Hartman, Moskal, and Dziuban 2005, 6.1). Educators have a responsibility to work to turn these challenges into opportunities.

According to Joel Hartman, Patsy Moskal, and Chuck Dziuban some challenges arise from students' comparison of colleges' online services with the top online commercial sites, such as Amazon or Google (2005). Thus, the Millennials are the least satisfied, compared to generations before them, with their college experience. They are wired and wireless and are expecting the same level of customer service, style, and satisfaction from their college or university as they get from Amazon or Google. Furthermore, Millennial students have access to multifunctional devices, such as cell phones equipped with cameras and Web browsers, that can play videos and music as well as receive e-mail and text messages. These devices support their need for interpersonal communication and connection. This generation views technology and its devices as platforms for "socializing, communicating, staying connected, playing games, and learning" (Turkle 1995, 60). In addition, Millennials have also rushed to use technologies like blogs, wikis, podcasts, IM, text messaging, and social networking sites; college campuses; however, have not, for the most part, integrated these technology tools into the core infrastructure of their campuses (Hartman, Moskal, and Dziuban 2005). Rather, colleges and universities often use low-level technologies to help with classroom instruction—overhead projectors, televisions, and video players, for example, are common in the classroom.

On the other hand, during the past fifteen to twenty years, many colleges and universities have moved technology to the forefront of their budgetary considerations. Technology is no longer considered a one-time expenditure; instead, it has been awarded a permanent budget line. New educational buildings and residence halls are built with technology in mind, all provide hardwired or wireless for high-speed Internet access. The question is no longer if colleges and universities will offer access to technology but rather how to make technology more accessible to students (Clayton-Pedersen and O'Neill 2005). Colleges and universities must provide wired and wireless buildings, computer labs, and laptops, thus creating access virtually everywhere on campus. Unfortunately, the current situation is that the technology available to the students often connects with them outside of the classroom and absent professors. There is thus a relationship between the students and the faculty and between the students and the technology; not, however, among all three. By developing this triad relationship, Millennial students will be more engaged and will more readily learn the proper and ethical use of technology and the information gleaned from it.

Millennials & the Library

Libraries play a critical role in the education of students and are perhaps in the best position to integrate learning and technology. They purchase databases that provide electronic access to either full-text articles or citations; they provide collections of organized resources, both print and electronic; and they offer in-person and virtual assistance to help students with their information needs. In addition, libraries also provide direct learning related to course work, such as group or one-on-one instruction. So, why are libraries still not connected to many of today's Millennial students?

One of the most cited reasons is students' dependence upon Google and other search engines (Lippincott 2005). Studies have shown repeatedly that students use Google first to gather resources for their papers. In fact, in a recent study conducted at Colorado State University, researchers found that 58 percent of freshmen used Google as their first choice for research, while only 23 percent started with a database (Kaminski, Seel, and Collen 2003, 38). Students often find that subscription databases purchased by the library are more difficult to understand than Google, and students are often not engaged in any bibliographic instruction sessions offered in their classes. Thus they prefer the simplicity of Google and other search engines. "Students may perceive that librarians have developed systems that are complex and make sense to information professionals but are too difficult to use without being an expert" (Online Computer Library Center 2002, 9). In addition, not all subscription databases contain full-text information, whereas a Google search usually yields full-text in one link or another. When it does not, they simply click the next link, or, surprisingly, frustrated students come to the library complaining about the link not working. Millennials are concerned with speed and the full gratification of their information needs when and where they needed it.

Educators are frustrated by students continued use of information obtained from the Web, often without verifying sources or choosing suitable scholarly resources. At Southwestern University, a team of IT professionals, librarians, and faculty developed a survey that was based upon the National Academies'[2] fluency with information technology principles and the ACRL Information Literacy Competency Standards (McEuen 2001). They found that students rated themselves highly when it came to finding information on the Internet, but these students rated themselves much lower when it came to finding resources appropriate to their research, i.e. scholarly publications. It is clear that librarians will have to be concerned with developing content, services, and environments in which Millennial students can achieve desired academic outcomes.

2.   The National Academies is an organization comprised of the National Academy of Sciences, the National Academy of Engineering, the Institute of Medicine, and the National Research Council.

3 SRU Research Project: Purpose, Design, and Methodology

Bailey Library of Slippery Rock University has always worked to pro-actively help students by providing library instruction sessions, online tutorials, and one-on-one assistance, covering topics ranging from general library orientation to more specific disciplinary advanced research. The library faculty at Bailey Library, as in many academic libraries, have long debated the value of various methods of library instruction and the suitability of different methodologies for different groups of students and different purposes. Within the library profession, many assume that friendly, personal contact with students at an early point in their academic careers breaks down barriers. However, many posit that the Millennial generation, and probably future generations, learn best through the use of technological tools. The purpose of this research project was to avoid speculation by testing the effectiveness of various treatment methods available for helping freshmen overcome library anxiety. After determining the most effective method for easing library anxiety in first-year students, faculty at Bailey Library intend to use those methodologies that best alleviate student anxiety.

The research team had three specific aims and objectives for their research project.

1. Measure levels of library anxiety in freshmen students;
2. Determine the most effective method(s) of easing library anxiety;
3. Implement the method(s) as a means of lowering anxiety in future students.

These aims and objectives were little changed as the project developed.

To measure student anxiety, the research team chose Sharon Bostick's Library Anxiety Scale, which was used to test both pre-treatment and post-treatment levels of library anxiety. Using the scale, library anxiety levels were tested near the beginning of the semester and again toward the end of the semester, with the treatment taking place in between. Bostick designed, tested, and validated the Library Anxiety Scale in the early 1990s, and it has been used in many studies to measure levels of library anxiety. This instrument includes forty-three statements that require responses along a five-point Likert scale. Items on the scale cover five dimensions of library anxiety: library staff, confidence in library use, comfort with the library, knowledge of the library, and use of mechanical components within the library. In addition, the research team gathered demographic data using three questions at the end of the assessment. This data included gender, major, and average annual visits to the library. With a proven track record and a strong reputation, the research team felt that the Library Anxiety Scale would best suit the project.

The research project, which began as a semester-long project, snowballed into a three-year study. During that time, some logistical changes were necessary—participants were recruited differently and treatment groups were restructured. As the research team became more acquainted with the topic and the research methodology, the process was refined and a smoother method of information gathering was developed. First launched in the fall of the 2005/2006 academic year, the project continued in the fall of the 2006/2007 and the fall of 2007/2008 academic years.

Year One (2005/06)

The first year of the study served as a pilot project that enabled the research team to work out kinks in the study design; the data collected was not used in final analysis.

Treatment Methods Tested

Originally the research team tested five treatment methods for easing library anxiety. These methods included:

1. Online tutorial,
2. Group library instruction (traditional classroom instruction),
3. One-on-one instruction,
4. Group library instruction followed by an online tutorial,
5. No Instruction of any kind (control group).[3]

---

3.   When the control group was finished with their part of the research project, library instruction was provided. We felt that completely excluding them would be detrimental to their academic achievement.

The research team hypothesized that Group 3 (one-on-one instruction) and Group 4 (group instruction followed by an online tutorial) would experience the greatest decrease in library anxiety.

Participants

Year one of the examined only first-year students in the College of Business, Information, and Social Sciences (CBISS). The Dean of the College, Dr. Bruce Russell, was interested in the research and offered financial support; this professional and financial support made students in this school our obvious choice. Catherine Rudowsky, a co-author of this book, also serves as the library liaison to the School of Business and the Social Work and Criminology & Criminal Justice Department, two departments within CBISS. We knew that these established relationships would undoubtedly lead to a higher rate of compliance.

The research team randomly chose one hundred freshmen CBISS majors from a list of 232 fall 2005 freshmen CBISS majors provided by the registrar. During the summer of 2005, these one hundred students received a letter at their home addresses asking them to participate in the research project. Participation was completely voluntary; small gifts; however, were offered as an enticement. These included five dollar coffee shop gift cards for each participant, and two twenty-five dollar campus bookstore gift cards to be drawn from all participants post-study. All participants had to be eighteen years of age or older in order to facilitate IRB approval. IRB protocol also required signed consent forms of all participants; all students willingly complied. Originally, the research team anticipated that fifty to one hundred students would participate. Unfortunately, the response rate was much lower, and the sample size in 2005 was only eighteen students. These eighteen students were randomly divided, as evenly as possible, between the five treatment groups listed above.

Administration

Near the beginning of the fall 2005 semester, student participants received details of the study design and the following outlined of expectations:

1. Complete the Library Anxiety Scale at a set time during the first week of October;
2. Complete the specific task(s) of the treatment group to which they were assigned;

3. Complete the Library Anxiety Scale at a set time during the first week of December.

The Scale was administered during the first week of October, after students had completed one month of classes. This delay allowed students time to formulate opinions regarding the library. After completing the pre-treatment library anxiety scale, but prior to completing the post-treatment scale, each group completed one of the following tasks:

Group 1   These students completed the online information literacy tutorial found on the library web page. This tutorial consists of three modules, each lasting approximately 30 minutes.

Group 2   These students participated in a group library instruction session lasting approximately 50 minutes. Sessions were conducted by one of the nine librarians on staff. A checklist was used to ensure that the same basic material was covered in each session. Most students encountered these sessions naturally as part of their College Writing I class. If they were not scheduled for any library instruction in any of their classes, they had to contact someone from the research team to arrange to sit in on a session.

Group 3   These students completed a one-on-one library instruction session lasting approximately 50 minutes. Either Martina Malvasi or Catherine Rudowsky, two members of the research team, conducted the sessions. A checklist was used to ensure that the same basic material was being covered in each session.

Group 4   These students completed both a group library instruction session (see Group 2 above) and the online information literacy tutorial (see Group 1 above).

Group 5   Students in this group had to purposefully avoid library instruction in any format, including in person and online, since these students served as the control group.

All students were reminded that they could not participate in library instruction, either in person or online, prior to the first week of October, and students in Group 5 were instructed that they could not participate in any library instruction, either in person or online, until the completion of the project. Furthermore, students in Groups 2 and 3 could not complete any part of the online information literacy tutorial prior to the conclusion of the research project, and students in Groups 1 and 3 could not participate in group library instruction prior to the conclusion of the research project. If students were asked to participate in library instruction as part of course work, they were asked to immediately contact a research team member who in turn contacted the student's instructor and explained the situation asking that the student be excused. Faculty were assured that instruction would be provided at the conclusion of the project. The research team readministered the Library Anxiety Scale during the first week of December to test post-treatment levels of library anxiety. This late date in the semester allowed the control group to experience the library independently, making it possible to test for a natural reduction in library anxiety as the result of completing a semester of college.

Administration of the Library Anxiety Scale and the group instruction sessions took place at Bailey Library in the instruction classroom. The one-on-one library instruction sessions took place in either Martina Malvasi's or Catherine Rudowsky's offices. Those taking the online tutorial were permitted to do so from any computer, and the control group was given no specific instruction to persuade them to use or not use the library. The research team, however, hoped that they would use the library on their own.

Analysis of the Data

Given that our independent variables were categorical variables, our study used an analysis of variance approach (ANOVA) to discern whether or not the sample means of these sub-populations changed in any statistically significant way after being subjected to different treatments. Using data on other determinants, such as age, gender and number of library visits, allow us to perform two and even three-way Analysis of Variance.

Year Two (2006/07) & Year Three (2007/08)

During the 2005/06 project, the research team noted limitations and gained experience. Limitations included a small sample size, lack of consistent contact with student participants, and a lack of control over such critical factors as ensuring that the online tutorial was actually completed. In the first year of the study we had no way of ascertaining if a student actually completed the tutorial, a huge concern in hindsight. Given what we learned, the research team decided to replicate the project with changes.

Treatment Methods Tested

In order to make the research more manageable and in order to provide groups with relatively the same time commitments, the research team decided to eliminate the combination of group instruction and the online tutorial and test only four treatment methods:

1. Online tutorial
2. No instruction of any kind (control group)
3. One-on-one library instruction
4. Group library instruction

The parameters for these groups did not change from the first year. Students were divided as equally as possible among the four groups and participated in accordance with the 2005/06 guidelines.

Participants

The team wished to increase the size of the sample and make the recruitment of participants less dependent upon random volunteers. Faculty in four FYRST seminar classes[4] agreed to ask their students to be part of the study. Although students still participated on a voluntary basis, the research team believed they would achieve a higher rate of compliance because they could have closer contact with and monitoring of students. Librarians introduced the project to them in a regular class period, and as a class, randomly assigned them to one of the four treatment groups.

4. The FYRST Seminar is a one-credit course designed specifically for first year students. The goal of the FYRST seminar is to assist students in their adjustment to college life. It provides students with an opportunity to participate in the University community by utilizing campus programs, services and technology. Students are introduced to their major, if enrolled in a FYRST seminar related to their major, and learn to develop their academic skills and learning strategies. Students in FYRST seminars are often brought to the library as a class for an orientation and introductory instruction.

In 2006/07, most students had majors in communication, computer science, criminal justice, or were undeclared, as these were the primary majors in the FYRST classes involved. Each FYRST class included twenty to twenty-five students, for a total of eighty to one hundred possible participants. Students could opt out at their discretion, and, as before, students under eighteen could not participate. At the end of the project, the usable sample size included seventy-two students.

In 2007/08, most students had majors in communication, exercise science, therapeutic recreation, or were undeclared. All other conditions remained the same as the previous year. At the end of the project, the usable sample size included seventy-one students.

Administration

In addition to changes in treatment methods tested and the recruitment of participants, the timeline for years two and three was slightly different because of the need to consider FYRST faculty schedules. Students in all of the groups completed the pre-survey during September instead of October. Students, unfortunately, had less time to form an opinion of the university library, but they were also less likely to encounter library instruction. The post-survey was completed near the end of November, prior to Thanksgiving recess. Given this timeframe, the control group had slightly less than an entire semester to experience a natural reduction in anxiety.

Statistical Methodology

As is well documented in Chapter 2, previous studies of library anxiety have used questionnaires in order to ascertain a supposed level of anxiety residing in the person responding to some aspect of library use. Lacking a physiological measure of a person's level of anxiety, such as a physician has when, for example, measuring a person's blood pressure, a questionnaire becomes an approximation at best. Most if not all questionnaires used in the study of library anxiety, such as Bostick's Library Anxiety Scale, offer respondents five different responses to questions or statements: 'strongly agree', 'agree', 'uncertain', 'disagree', or 'strongly disagree'. If we assume that anxiety is a continuous variable and as such there exists an infinite number of possible levels of anxiety, using five possible responses is at best an imprecise way to discriminate between the differences in anxiety levels of those examined. Though admittedly imprecise, to date no better methods exist; unless and until a mechanical instrument is found, we will continue to use such ordinal approximations.

Measuring Library Anxiety – the Scaling Problem

Even if we assume that using five different responses to a question can effectively reproduce five different levels of anxiety, the problem as to how much anxiety lies between one response and another is still left unanswered. How much more or less anxiety does a person responding 'strongly disagree' to a question have compared to someone responding 'disagree' to the same question? Assigning numbers as measures of anxiety to different responses intimates that we know those differences and introduces a degree of error that in the final analysis may do more harm than good.

Measuring Library Anxiety – the Aggregation Problem

Can the level of anxiety on a particular dimension of library use be added to the level of anxiety on another dimension of library use? In other words, are anxieties additive or do they instead interact in ways that do not allow us to add or subtract levels of anxiety on different dimensions of library use? This question is pertinent to this study because we propose to measure levels of library anxiety along the five different dimensions established by Sharon Bostick: 1) Barriers with Staff, 2) Affective Barriers, 3) Comfort with the Library, 4) Knowledge of the Library, and 5) Mechanical Barriers.

If one assumes that anxiety is additive, it is theoretically possible to end up with a person having zero anxiety, simply because the sum of the anxiety levels exhibited in some dimensions cancel out the sum of negative anxiety levels in other dimensions.[5] This result is of course unacceptable simply because that person does have anxiety and enjoy-

---

5. A system that attaches anxiety values to the different responses in the questionnaire ends up using at least one negative number to one of the five responses. For example when a person is asked to respond to a question that reflects negatively on the library, the response 'disagree' should equate to 'no anxiety'. If so, the response 'strongly disagree' should equate with a negative level of anxiety. Likewise, a similar negative anxiety value should be associated with the response 'strongly agree' if the question reflects positively on some aspect of library use.

ing some aspects of the library should not offset anxiety arising from other aspects of library use.

In conclusion, inferences made from models where anxiety levels are assigned sequential values and then used to fit linear regression models (LRM) can lead to misleading conclusions. In the words of J. Scott Long (1997, 115):

> Researchers often, and perhaps usually, treat ordinal dependent variables as if they were interval. The dependent categories are numbered sequentially and the LRM is used. This involves the implicit assumption that the intervals between adjacent categories are equal. For example, the distance between strongly agreeing and agreeing is assumed to be the same distance between agreeing and being neutral on a Likert scale. Winship and Mare (1984) review the debate between those who argue that the ease of use, simple interpretation, and flexibility of the LRM justify its use with ordinal outcomes versus those who argue that the bias introduced by regression of an ordinal variable makes this practice unacceptable. Both McKelvey and Zavoina (1975, p.117) and Winship and Mare (1984, pp.521-523) give examples where regression of an ordinal outcome provides misleading results. Given this risk, prudent researchers should use models specifically designed for ordinal variables.

In the next section, we propose using an Ordered-Logit model that we believe resolves satisfactorily the scaling and aggregation problems alluded to in this section.

The Ordered Logit Model

The Ordered Logit Model (OLM) was designed specifically to make inferences from ordinal level data such as the one gathered for this study during the fall of 2006 and the fall of 2007. The OLM is, however, a probabilistic model; it makes no attempt to measure anxiety directly, instead it measures indirectly by trying to discriminate among individuals who seem inclined to choose one of the ordinal choices as opposed to the others. The OLM accomplishes this by computing a value that is a function of the independent variables, which the researcher believes are key determinants of how individuals feel regarding the questions being asked of them (called a latent function). The OLM then determines the statistical significance of the explanatory variables being used and, in a sense, either lends support or not to the researcher's theory regarding the importance of the variables included as independent variables.

If the explanatory variables chosen are statistically significant then a significant correlation exists between the latent function so constructed and the selection of choices offered the respondents. For example, when for a particular individual the latent function takes on values that are extreme (relative to all other values of the function), the probability the individual selects an extreme choice such as 'strongly agree' or 'strongly disagree' is correspondingly high.[6] More moderate values of the latent function should equate with a higher probability that the individual selects more moderate choices such as 'agree', or 'disagree', or 'uncertain'.

The advantages of the OLM are substantial. First, it avoids any scaling problem simply because it never seeks to measure anxiety directly. It does this by assuming that the latent function and the individual's level of anxiety are both continuous limitless functions and that an implicit one-to-one relationship exists between the two. The OLM, however, must identify critical values on the latent function, which signal when an individual is more likely to switch to a different ordered choice. The OLM estimates these so called cut-off points along with the coefficients for the explanatory variables included in the model. A simultaneous estimation of all coefficients takes place by maximizing the likelihood that all individuals sampled will select the choices they actually did select.

The OLM also avoids the aggregation problem. With no anxiety measures the aggregation problem is never encountered. The researcher can add probabilities, but these of course, must adhere to the established laws for adding probabilities.

---

6. The latent function is a continuous function that theoretically ranges from negative infinity to positive infinity. It is called a latent function because it is neither observable nor does it lend itself to interpretation, since it is constructed as a linear combination of variables that are distinct not only in meaning but in level of measurement – such as gender, major, number of library visits, and treatment group.

C4 Results & Discussion

In this chapter we present the results on the effectiveness of treatments in reducing library anxiety both for the 2006 and 2007 surveys. The effectiveness of a treatment was measured by the Ordered Logit Model (OLM) as the impact the treatment had on a group's probability of reducing library anxiety. These probabilities were computed for the full samples as representative of the population of newly accepted college freshmen students and for sub-samples composed of students the OLM selected as having shown relatively higher anxiety during the pre-treatment phase of the study.

We first present the results of the treatments' effectiveness on overall library anxiety broken down by sample size and then show the effectiveness of treatments on each one of the five dimensions of library anxiety as determined by Sharon Bostick (1992). We follow these results by presenting the correlations obtained between the probability of reducing library anxiety and the control variables: gender, the student's major, and the student's average annual visits to a library. We wrap up by presenting our conclusions regarding which methods of treatment are more effective when dealing with freshman students in general and when dealing with freshman students that have been identified as having relatively greater levels of library anxiety.

Focusing on High Anxiety Students – Reduced Samples

The research team thought it would be of interest to examine how the effectiveness of treatments fared when applied only to students with higher levels of library anxiety. To do so, students who showed very little overall anxiety during the pre-treatment phase of the studies were eliminated from the full samples. For obvious reasons, these students had very little to gain from treatments designed to reduce anxiety.

The following decisions were made with regard to how many students were to be eliminated in order to arrive at sub-samples composed of higher anxiety students:

A. Low anxiety students were defined as those having a high probability of selecting either choice "N" (Negative anxiety) or choice 'Z' (Zero anxiety) as responses to the statements on the pre-survey phase of the studies. Using probability laws, the probability of selecting choices 'N' or 'Z' on question 'i' was defined as:

$$\Pr('N_i' \text{ or } 'Z_i') = \Pr('N_i') + \Pr('Z_i') + \Pr('N_i' \text{ and } 'Z_i')$$

$$= \Pr('N_i') + \Pr('Z_i')$$

The last term drops out simply because choices 'N' and 'Z' are mutually exclusive. The overall probability that a student would select either choice 'N' or choice 'Z' was defined as the average of the corresponding probabilities on all questions. That is:

$$\Pr('N' \text{ or } 'Z') = \frac{\sum_{i=1}^{43} \Pr('N_i' \text{ or } 'Z_i')}{43}$$

This probability measure was used to rank all students from low anxiety to high anxiety.

B. The same percentage of low pre-survey anxiety students were dropped from each treatment group as opposed to dropping students with anxiety probabilities below a certain threshold. The latter method unfortunately dropped too many students from some groups while dropping few or none from the other groups. Initially, 25 percent of the lowest anxiety students were dropped from each group. An analysis of the effectiveness of treatment was performed on the remaining 75 percent. This same process was repeated, but this time eliminating approximately 35 percent of students with low pre-survey anxiety probabilities. Larger reductions were not possible; it was discovered through trial and error that the Ordered Logit Model (OLM) understandably failed to achieve convergence on some questions when the sample size used for estimation was reduced by 38 percent or more of the full sample. The effectiveness of treatment on these high anxiety students can be seen on Graphs 4.1 through 4.6 and are denoted as having lower values for the sample size parameter N. The raw data used to create Graphs 4.1 through 4.6 can be found in Tables 2 and 3 of appendix B.

Overall Library Anxiety

Graph 4.1 illustrates the probability by treatment group by sample size of reducing overall library anxiety.

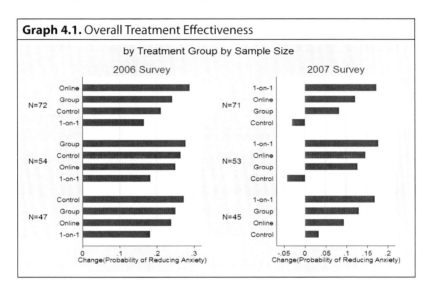

Graph 4.1. Overall Treatment Effectiveness

Full Sample

In 2006, for the full sample of seventy-two students, the Online Tutorial proved to be the most effective at reducing overall library anxiety. This was followed by Group Instruction, the Control Group, and One-on-One Instruction. In 2007, for the full sample of seventy-one students, the ranking were One-on-One Instruction, Online Tutorial, and Group Instruction followed lastly by the Control Group. In this instance, the Control Group actually experienced a negative change or increase in library anxiety.

An analysis of the full samples from both 2006 and 2007 revealed that some intervention is better than no intervention. The Online Tutorial, in particular, presents itself as a strong option for reducing library anxiety having ranked first in 2006 and second in 2007. On the other hand, the Control Group, or no intervention, presents itself as the least effective means of reducing library anxiety having ranked next to last in 2006 and last in 2007. Group Instruction and One-on-One Instruction are less consistent in their rankings, particularly One-on-One Instruction, which jumped from last place in 2006 to first place in 2007.

A possible explanation for the greater volatility in the effectiveness of some treatments is that their effectiveness may very well be affected by variables beyond our control. Two variables that affected all treatment groups in any given year are associated with the students themselves and the FYRST instructors[7]. The general attitude of students and their openness to learning new things is uncontrollable. This becomes more evident later in this chapter when evidence is presented illustrating that the level of library anxiety related to Affective Barriers, a measure of student confidence, was drastically different between 2006 and 2007. Students, in addition, were different individually across years and within years. Individual student use of the library outside of this project was beyond our control. Almost certainly each of these students used the library to different degrees on different schedules encountering different librarians and staff. In addition to student differences, each group had a different FYRST instructor. This was true across years and within years. Each of the four groups within a given year, obviously, had different FYRST instructors, and different FYRST instructors were used in 2006 and 2007, except for one. How these instructors reacted to the project, the amount of time they spent discussing the library, and their general attitude toward the library could well have differed. The effects of these unknowns were not only uncontrollable; their impact on the students' behavior was immeasurable.

Treatment methods can also be affected by other variables. Group Instruction and One-on-One Instruction have in particular an added effect deriving from the person providing the library instruction. The same librarian, whether in a group setting or a one-on-one setting, did not provide all instruction. This was true both outside of our project and within our project. In 2006, for example, Ms. Rudowsky provided group library instruction while in 2007 Ms. Malvasi provided group library instruction. Both Ms. Rudowsky and Ms. Malvasi provided all one-on-one instruction in 2006 and 2007, dividing the responsibility equally. There is no guarantee that various instructors prove to be as

7.   As explained in chapter 4, the FYRST Seminar is a one-credit course designed specifically for first year students to assist in adjustment to college life. Four different FYRST Seminar classes were used in both 2006 and 2007 to provide participants for the study. Each of the classes were taught by different instructors.

effective at reducing library anxiety, and for that matter, there is no guarantee that any one instructor is as effective on one day as he or she is on another. The human element means there are days when instructors are at their best and days when they are not as effective. The same, of course, can be said of students. And, when instruction is provided in only one session, this effect could be significant. In this case, there is only a fifty-minute window of opportunity for effectively reducing library anxiety within the participants. The online tutorial, on the other hand, is devoid of the instructor effect and is, therefore, more likely to be consistent in its effectiveness from year to year.

Reduced Samples

As low anxiety students were eliminated, changes in the order of effectiveness among treatment methods were observed. Group Instruction, for these reduced samples, proved to be the most effective at easing library anxiety, having ranked first or second a majority of the time across all samples in both years. The Online Tutorial, however, was no longer the most effective option, ranking second only once across all samples in both years. In fact, it most consistently ranked third, proving to be one of the least effective treatment methods. Among higher anxiety students, the Control Group and One-on-One Instruction lacked consistency. The Control Group ranked first or second across samples in 2006, yet it ranked last across samples in 2007. One-on-One Instruction, as with the full sample, ranked last twice in 2006 and first twice in 2007.

The reduced effectiveness of Online Instruction among high anxiety students can be explained several ways. The more anxious a student is, the more confusing and overwhelming information can be without the personal touch and comfort of a human instructor. An instructor can appropriately gear different instruction sessions to different groups of students based on skills ranging from reading body language and facial expressions to verbal communication and cues. The Online Tutorial, furthermore, leaves students alone feeling isolated and leaving them to foster the belief that everyone else surely understands the information while they are not. Having peers around could eliminate this feeling of isolation. The increased effectiveness of the Group Instruction method in such cases supports the notion that having a human instructor and the support of peers increases the effectiveness of group instruction when dealing with highly anxious students with low levels of confidence. The extreme and opposite ranking of the Control Group and One-on-One Instruction among highly anxious students in 2006 and 2007 can best be explained by the variables discussed above under the full sample.

The Five Dimensions of Library Anxiety

To gain further insight on library anxiety, it was of interest to determine the sources giving rise to library anxiety and whether or not these causes were similarly distributed across samples and across time. In addition to overall anxiety, analysis was performed on the effectiveness of the various treatment methods to reduce anxiety related to each of the five dimensions as defined by Sharon Bostick (1992). These are barriers with staff, affective barriers, comfort with the library, knowledge of the library, and mechanical barriers.

Where Anxiety Resides[8]

In 2006 mechanical barriers caused the most anxiety, followed by comfort with the library, barriers with staff, affective barriers, and knowledge of the library. In 2007 library anxiety related to mechanical barriers was again highest, followed by affective barriers, comfort with the library, barriers with staff, and knowledge of the library. The rankings did not change in either 2006 or 2007 as the sample size was reduced.

Both years were consistent in that students experienced the greatest anxiety in relationship to mechanical barriers, that is, the use of technology and equipment ranging from printers to photocopy machines. This was somewhat surprising considering that the sample population consisted of Millennials, a generation that has grown up with technology and equipment being as common as paper and pencil. Both years were also consistent in that the source of least anxiety related to knowledge of the library, which refers to how familiar students are with using the library. Again, this was somewhat surprising, as the team assumed that the difference between using a school library and an academic library was at the heart of the anxiety. Both barriers with staff, which refers

8. The percentage of responses indicating some degree of anxiety (choices L (low), M (medium), and H (high) was computed for every one of the five dimensions of library anxiety. This percentage was used to rank these dimensions from most causing to least causing sources of anxiety.

Table 4.1. Causes of Library Anxiety Ranked Most to Least

2006		
N=72	**N=54**	**N=47**
Mechanical Barriers	Mechanical Barriers	Mechanical Barriers
Comfort with the Library	Comfort with the Library	Comfort with the Library
Barriers with Staff	Barriers with Staff	Barriers with Staff
Affective Barriers	Affective Barriers	Affective Barriers
Knowledge of the Library	Knowledge of the Library	Knowledge of the Library
2007		
N=71	**N=53**	**N=45**
Mechanical Barriers	Mechanical Barriers	Mechanical Barriers
Affective Barriers	Affective Barriers	Affective Barriers
Comfort with the Library	Comfort with the Library	Comfort with the Library
Barriers with Staff	Barriers with Staff	Barriers with Staff
Knowledge of the Library	Knowledge of the Library	Knowledge of the Library

to student perception of librarians and library staff, and comfort with the library, which refers to how safe and welcome students feel in the library, showed very little change, staying firmly in the middle in both 2006 and 2007. Affective barriers, which refer to feelings of inadequacy, was most unstable ranking last in 2006 but second in 2007.

Barriers with Staff

Anxiety associated with barriers with staff, which refers to student perception of the librarians and staff, was most effectively treated in the Online Tutorial Group for the full sample in 2006. This was followed by Group Instruction, the Control Group, and One-on-One Instruction. In 2007, it was most effectively treated with One-on-One Instruction followed by the Online Tutorial, Group Instruction and the Control Group.

These results and rankings are unchanged from the results found when looking at the full sample for overall library anxiety. Again, for the full sample, the Online Tutorial proved most effective, ranking first in

2006 and second in 2007, while the Control Group ranked last or next to last both years. Also the same, One-on-One Instruction and Group Instruction were less consistent, particularly One-on-One Instruction, which was again least effective in 2006 and most effective in 2007. The influence of uncontrollable factors originating from the students' effort, the FYRST instructors' impact, and the library instructors' effectiveness can be used here to explain the volatility of the One-on-One and Group Instruction treatments just as it was used in explaining the full sample results for overall anxiety.

Graph 4.2 also shows that changes in the effectiveness of treatments occurred as low anxiety students were eliminated. Group Instruction became the most effective, ranking first or second across all samples in both years. The Online Tutorial on the other hand was clearly the least effective, ranking last or next to last across all samples in both years. It should be noted that the effectiveness of Online Instruction and the Control Group were not statistically different in 2006 for N=54. The Control Group ranked second in 2006 and last in 2007, while One-on-One Instruction ranked last in 2006 but first in 2007. These findings were again closely aligned with the findings for the reduced samples in overall library anxiety. Again, the reduced effectiveness of the Online Tutorial and the increased effectiveness of Group Instruction can be explained by the notion that the more anxious a student is the more they benefit from the personal touch and comfort of a human instructor while benefiting from having peers nearby to help eliminate any feelings of inadequacy.

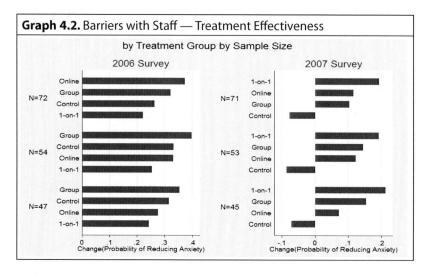

Graph 4.2. Barriers with Staff — Treatment Effectiveness

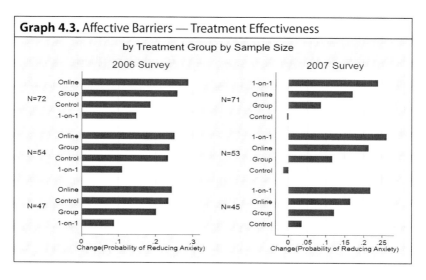

Graph 4.3. Affective Barriers — Treatment Effectiveness

Affective Barriers

In both 2006 and 2007 for the full sample, anxiety related to affective barriers, which refers to feelings of inadequacy when using the library, yielded identical results as were obtained for overall library anxiety and anxiety related to barriers with staff.

Again, the Online Tutorial was the most effective, the Control Group was the least effective, and One-on-One Instruction experienced a drastic change, moving from least effective in 2006 to most effective in 2007. Here again we can argue that the influence of uncontrollable factors originating from the students' effort, the FYRST instructors' impact, and the library instructors' effectiveness can be used to explain the volatility of the One-on-One and Group Instruction treatments.

Eliminating low anxiety students, however, presented changes that proved different from both overall library anxiety and barriers with staff. The Online Tutorial performed the best yet among high anxiety students ranking first or second across all samples in both years. Group Instruction was least effective ranking next to last three out of four times. These findings are opposite those previously discussed in which Group Instruction was the most effective treatment method among high anxiety students and the Online Tutorial was the least effective. The Control Group changed little, and One-on-One Instruction remained exactly the same, again ranking least effective in 2006 and most effective in 2007.

Affective barriers can be thought of as being inversely related to a student's level of confidence. Students with high levels of anxiety related to affective barriers feel inadequate when compared to their peers, and, therefore, can be presumed to have low levels of confidence. The increased effectiveness of the Online Tutorial and the reduced effectiveness of Group Instruction derive from the possibility that students with low levels of confidence are intimidated by a group setting. In a group setting these low confidence students worry that their weaknesses are more likely to be exposed. The Online Tutorial, on the other hand, allows students to remain anonymous, evade human contact, and avoid judgment.

Comfort with the Library

Anxiety related to comfort with the library, which refers to how safe and comfortable students feel in the library, presented consistent results when compared to previous analyses for the full sample. The Online Tutorial, for example, was the most effective, and One-on-One Instruction experienced a drastic change, moving from least effective in 2006 to most effective in 2007. Other differences, however, were also observed. The Control Group was not the least effective, having ranked second in 2006 but remaining last in 2007. This is the first time in our analysis that it does not rank last or next to last in both 2006 and 2007. Group Instruction, on the other hand, was the least effective ranking next to last in both 2006 and 2007.

Overall, the same consistent pattern of results emerges whenever the full sample is considered. The Online Tutorial was most effective and

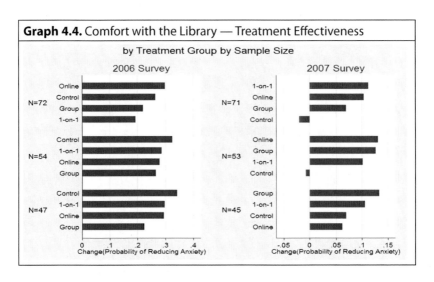

Graph 4.4. Comfort with the Library — Treatment Effectiveness

One-on-One Instruction was the most volatile, while Group Instruction and the Control Group were least effective. This pattern of results can be explained by applying the same notions as before, namely that variables such as students, FYRST instructors, and library instructors are pertinent and uncontrollable from year to year.

In the samples focusing on higher anxiety students, One-on-One Instruction was the most effective having ranked first or second a majority of the time across all samples in both years. This was the only time across all dimensions that One-on-One Instruction ranked most effective among high anxiety students. It is worth noting, however, that the effectiveness of One-on-One Instruction was not statistically different from that of the Online Tutorial in 2006 for N=47. The Online Tutorial, on the other hand, was the least effective and most consistently ranked next to last across samples and years. The Control Group and Group Instruction experienced the most volatility. The Control Group ranked first in 2006 yet last or next to last in 2007 while Group Instruction ranked last in 2006 yet first or second in 2007. A possible explanation for the fact that One-on-One Instruction did well in reducing library anxiety associated with the comfort of the library dimension is that comfort and safety are human emotions not easily understood or conveyed by a computer. Students are more likely to accept a message of safety and comfort in the library from a person whose job is to work in a library than from an online program.

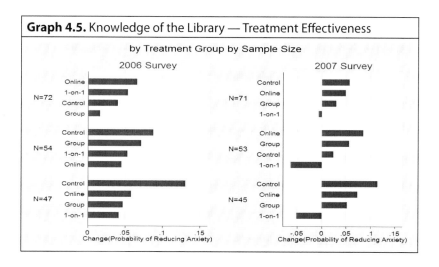

Graph 4.5. Knowledge of the Library — Treatment Effectiveness

Knowledge of the Library

Knowledge of the library, which refers to how familiar students are with using the library, presented some of the most unique results.

For the full sample, the Online Tutorial again was most effective having ranked first or second across both years. This is consistent with previous analyses. Group Instruction, as with comfort with the library but different from all other findings, was the least effective having ranked last or next to last across both years. Analysis of One-on-One Instruction and the Control Group presented the first unique findings under this dimension. One-on-One Instruction was more effective in 2006 than in 2007, while the Control Group was less effective in 2006 than in 2007. For all other dimensions, the opposite is true.

The elimination of low anxiety students also produced strange results. The Control Group performed its best, ranking as the most effective a majority of the time across all samples in both years. One-on-One Instruction did the worst, finishing as the least effective a majority of the time across all samples in both years.

It must be noted that all treatment methods showed the lowest probabilities of reducing anxiety caused by knowledge of the library. This is not surprising given that knowledge of the library ranked last as a source of library anxiety in both 2006 and 2007 (see table 4.1). Under these circumstances, any treatment method is likely to prove most or least effective under conditions of random sampling.

Mechanical Barriers

Treatment effectiveness for mechanical barriers, which refers to student use of mechanical equipment found in the library, aligned more closely with the pattern of results for overall anxiety and all dimensions of library anxiety excluding knowledge of the library when analyzing the general population.

As observed previously, when considering the general population of incoming freshmen students, the Online Tutorial was the most effective, the Control Group was the least effective, and Group Instruction was somewhere in the middle both in 2006 and 2007. One-on-One Instruction was the most volatile and drastically differed between 2006 and 2007, ranking as least effective in 2006 and then most effective in 2007. This consistent pattern of results can again be explained by con-

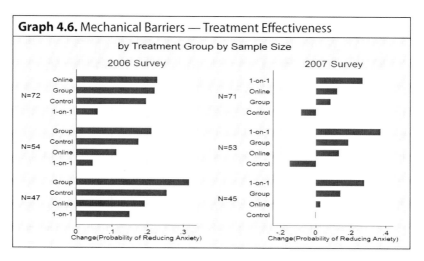

Graph 4.6. Mechanical Barriers — Treatment Effectiveness

by Treatment Group by Sample Size

sidering uncontrollable variables associated with the students' effort, inherent differences of FYRST instructors, and the use of different library instructors.

For samples focusing on high anxiety students, Group Instruction was the most effective having ranked first or second across all samples in both years. The Online Tutorial was the least effective having ranked next to last across all samples in both years. As seen before, the Control Group and One-on-One Instruction experienced the most volatility ranking at opposite ends of the spectrum across years. Again, the reduced effectiveness of the Online Tutorial and the increased effectiveness for Group Instruction can be explained by the idea that the more anxious a student is the more they benefit from the personal touch and comfort of a human instructor and from having peers nearby to help eliminate any feelings of inadequacy.

There are, however, problems in accurately analyzing mechanical barriers. Bostick's Library Anxiety Scale was created in 1992 and is dated regarding technology. Only three statements relate to mechanical barriers and none of these statements pertains to databases, online connectivity, or other current mechanical issues. Furthermore, having only three statements, to measure this dimension created problems. A slight change in the response rate of just one of the three questions making up this dimension can create drastically different results. This is not the case with the other dimensions, which were measured using five or more statements, and in the case of barriers with staff as many as fifteen statements.

Conclusions

Inferences Regarding the General Population of Incoming Freshmen

Analysis of the results demonstrates that some intervention is better than no intervention for reducing library anxiety in the general population of freshmen students. The Online Tutorial was clearly the most effective having consistently ranked first or second across both years for overall anxiety as well as for all five dimensions of library anxiety. The Control Group was the least effective having ranked last or next to last a majority of the time across both years for overall anxiety and for each of the five dimensions. Group Instruction appeared to be mediocre most often ranking in the middle, at second or third. One-on-One experienced the greatest volatility, regardless of the dimensions being analyzed, and drastically differed in its ranking from 2006 to 2007.

Inferences Regarding the Population of High Anxiety Students

Among high anxiety students, some intervention is again better than no intervention. Group Instruction was the most effective having ranked first or second when treating overall anxiety and also when treating each of the five dimensions of library anxiety across samples for both years. Among high anxiety students, the Online Tutorial was consistently the least effective treatment method ranking last or next to last across all samples in both years. The exception to this rule occurred when treating affective barriers and knowledge of the library sources of anxiety. The One-on-One Instruction method again showed a great deal of volatility both for the general population and among high anxiety students, making it difficult for us to draw any firm conclusions about its effectiveness.

Effects of Major, Gender, & Visits to the Library

Three outside influences were analyzed to determine their effects on the reduction of library anxiety: major, gender and the average number of visits to a library during a year.[9] This information was gathered as

9. The marginal effects of major, gender, and/or library visits were relatively small when compared to the effects of the treatments students were subjected to in order to reduce library anxiety. The effects of major, gender, and/or library visits were all below a 5 percent improvement or reduction in the ability to reduce library anxiety. The results stated here are only those that were consistent across both 2006 and 2007 and were statistically significant at a 90 percent or better level of confidence.

part of the Library Anxiety Scale and is recorded in appendix D. Again, the data was analyzed in terms of the full sample as well as the reduced samples intended to focus on higher anxiety students.

When analyzing data regarding majors, students were divided into two groups: those whose majors fell within the College of Business, Information, and Social Science (CBISS) and those whose majors fell within the other colleges on campus. For the full sample, CBISS majors appeared to have a slightly greater difficulty reducing overall library anxiety, anxiety related to comfort with the library, and anxiety related to knowledge of the library when compared to non-CBISS majors. Among high anxiety students, CBISS majors appeared to have a slightly greater difficulty reducing overall library anxiety as well as anxiety related to affective barriers, comfort with the library, and knowledge of the library when compared to non-CBISS majors.

Further analysis of demographics included gender comparisons. In the general population of freshmen students, females appeared to be better able to reduce anxiety related to barriers with staff when compared to male students. Female students, however, appeared to be less able to reduce anxiety related to mechanical barriers. Among high-anxiety students, females appeared to be better able to reduce anxiety related to affective barriers when compared to male students, yet again they appeared less able to reduce anxiety related to mechanical barriers.

The third outside influence was the student's experience visiting a library during a year. For the general population of freshmen students, those with less experience visiting a library appeared to have slightly greater ease in reducing anxiety related to comfort with the library than those who visit the library with greater frequency. Among high anxiety students, those with less experience visiting a library appeared to have a slightly greater difficulty reducing anxiety related to affective barriers.

The research team felt that offering explanations for why there are gender differences or major field of study differences or for that matter experience with library use differences in a student's ability to reduce library anxiety was beyond our expertise. We offer our findings merely as a point of interest and we thus leave it to our readers to draw their own conclusions.

5 Treatment Beyond Our Research

Interventions @ Bailey Library

As demonstrated in this and several other studies, library anxiety does in fact exist within the academic community. Students experience library anxiety on various levels, and it is important to address this issue and present possible solutions, in addition to instruction, to help minimize the anxiety that students experience. At Slippery Rock University, the librarians have initiated various programs and been involved in several campus initiatives in an effort to help create a less anxious learning environment.

FYRST Seminar

As part of a campus-wide initiative to assist students transitioning to college life, Slippery Rock University started a program called FYRST (First Year Studies). Dr. Amanda Yale, Associate Provost for Enrollment Services, brought this one-credit class, which is intended to assist freshmen in their transition to college life, to the campus. Topics offered range from stress management to underage drinking and its consequences. The library participates in FYRST Seminar on two levels. First, a librarian attends a summer FYRST Seminar workshop and makes a presentation to the FYRST Seminar faculty. This presentation is intended to provide information about library instruction and library tours are available to FYRST Seminar classes. Over the past three years, the library has seen a significant increase in the number of library instruction and tours conducted for FYRST Seminar classes. Secondly, librarians can teach a section of FYRST Seminar. This teaching opportunity puts a librarian in the classroom with direct student contact for a semester. Students become familiar, not only with a librarian, but also with how the library functions, thus helping to reduce the anxiety these students experience. These students often tell other students about their experience, and word often spreads about how helpful librarians are. This contact with students and other faculty allows the librarians to present a positive service model to the campus community. FYRST Seminar has provided a great opportunity to the librarians in reducing anxiety.

Faculty Fellows

Slippery Rock University also created Learning Communities in residence halls and an associated program called Faculty Fellows. These Learning Communities, which involve mostly freshmen and sophomore students, correspond to academic majors and disciplines offered on campus. One hall, for example, houses the Education Learning Community and the Honors Community, another houses the Frederick Douglas Leadership Community, and a third houses the Business, Information & Social Science Community. The Faculty Fellow portion of this program invites faculty from corresponding disciplines to work with the Learning Communities through activities and mentoring. Several librarians participate in the Faculty Fellows program. Catherine Rudowsky, one of the authors of this book and Business Librarian at SRU, is a Faculty Fellow to the CBISS (College of Business, Information, and Social Sciences) Learning Commons. Rudowsky attends regular meetings and participates in the various activities associated with her Learning Community. The Faculty Fellows program provides librarians a perfect opportunity to get to know students on a first name basis and, in turn, for students to get to know librarians. The more the librarians interact with students, the more likely these students are to visit the library and ask questions regarding their research and information needs. This direct student contact helps to reduce the library anxiety that most freshmen experience.

Public Relations & Social Events

Throughout the semester, Bailey Library offers special events for students, mixing in a bit of fun with academic pursuits. The idea is that students have an opportunity to interact with librarians in a friendly and non-intimidating manner. Students, who would not otherwise come to the library, participate in events and become fans of the library. Barriers and stereotypes are broken down, thus decreasing library anxiety. On Halloween, for example, the library hosts a guest speaker, followed by a light snack and midnight showing of a horror movie. Also well-received are the free candy bars librarians distribute in dining halls during midterm and finals week. The candy bars, wrapped in a special library wrapper that highlights library series, are always a hit. During National Library Week, the library holds a contest, with prizes that have ranged from a movie gift-basket filled with popular movies and movie treats, a cooking gift-basket filled with interesting cookbooks and supplies, to a bag of books gift-basket filled with a variety of current best sellers. The point of the contest is to provide students with a positive experience related to the library. Our most successful event is undoubtedly a study break during finals week. One evening early in that week, the library provides pizza, drinks, and a variety of sweets and treats to all who come. Students truly appreciate both the break and the food. Again, students see the librarians and the library staff in an entirely new way. Presenting a friendly and social face to students helps to lessen their anxiety and create a positive learning environment.

Academic Advisement

Because librarians at Slippery Rock University have faculty rank, they can serve as academic advisors. As academic advisors, librarians meet with students who have not yet declared a major and provide guidance regarding liberal studies courses. This provides another avenue for librarians to interact directly with students. Part of the advisement process includes talking to students about choosing a major and their current course work. Both of these topics provide a library teaching moment, as the librarian can provide tools and resources to assist students in researching a class or ways to search for information about a major. These advisement encounters bring students into the library, familiarize them with the Library, and help them become comfortable asking questions. This intervention serves several purposes as librarians work toward reducing library anxiety.

High School Visits

Melba Tomeo, Instructional Media Center Librarian, uses outreach to encourage teachers in neighboring school districts to bring their students to the library as part of a research day. Melba then engages students in the research process in a friendly, non-threatening environment in the hope that library anxiety can be reduced before students enter college. When younger students visit the library for a tour, they are treated to stories about the third-floor ghost, which grabs everyone's attention. Students no longer view the library as an intimidating place that seems painful to enter but instead as a place full of intrigue and mystery.

Intervention @ Libraries across the Country

In addition to the efforts being undertaken at Bailey Library, libraries across the country are reporting innovative efforts being employed to increase student comfort with the library.

LibraryFest

In an effort, for example, to help students recognize the value of library resources and services, the library staff at Millersville University of Pennsylvania created LibraryFest. They began with the concept that if students feel comfortable with the library on their own terms, they would begin to feel more comfortable using the library resources and services. Eventually these students would become more comfortable with the librarians and staff (Highman, Lutz, and Warmkessel 2007). Millersville University's library staff target LibraryFest to first-year students, but it is open to the entire university community. Enticing students with food, fun, and prizes, the library succeeds in creating a festive environment. The library staff create a "passport" system to encourage students to visit six selected stations in the library. Students visit each station, where their passports are punched and they collect a fact sheet that explained the resources and/or services available at that station. Library staff at each station also make themselves available for questions. A completely punched passport entitles students to a specially-designed mug and the opportunity to enter a drawing for a much bigger prize.

Millersville University held their first LibraryFest in 2004. All staff wore purple polo shirts and greeted visitors at the door with an explanation of the day's events. The following year the library added freshly grilled hotdogs to the line-up. In 2006, the library introduced "LibraryFest Olympics," an activity designed and coordinated by library student workers. During this event, passport stations included the Reference Desk, Circulation Desk, Government Documents, Special Collections, Curriculum Materials Center, Duplication Services, and General Stacks. The "LibraryFest Olympics" consisted of a golf putt using discarded books as boundaries, a book shuttle run, a cassette tape hockey shoot out, using discarded cassette tape cases, and a book truck race complete with orange cones.

In addition to all of the fun and activities, the library also provided students the opportunity to either draw or describe their ideal library. In direct response to student input, the library at Millersville University created two new seating areas with comfortable chairs and couches. In addition, some of the feedback was incorporated into the major renovation plan for Millersville University's library building.

Library Resources Course

Several universities, including Iowa State University, University of Maryland University College, and Indiana University of Pennsylvania, offer a for-credit course in library resources. These courses consist of modules that help students understand the library and the research process. Each module instructs students on different facets of research and contains assignments that reinforce information literacy. Some institutions require such a course for all students. This process ensures that all students are provided with library instruction on a more intense level than one fifty-minute bibliographic instruction session. These courses are typically one credit and can be completed in a seven-week schedule, thus allowing librarians to offer this course to more students each semester.

Library Ambassadors

In 2006, in response to student frustration in the libraries, McGill University in Canada started an outreach program they call Library Ambassadors. This group, which works in concert with the Students Society of McGill University (SSMU), is "a group of a dozen undergraduate students on a mission to make the complex familiar… Full-time undergraduates serve as points of contact for students, participate in orientation and other outreach activities, represent the Library at various campus events, refer students to professional library staff or provide basic help and liaise with student groups on library needs" (Gales 2006, 6). The librarians at McGill University have found that "being introduced to the Library by other students is a great initial point of contact for new students arriving at McGill" (Gale 2006, 6). The Library Ambassadors also take the message beyond the library walls and encourage students across campus to use the resources and services that are offered in the library.

A Luau in the Library

A truly innovative idea, library luau, conceived by Penn State University Libraries, provides a new twist to library orientation. Instead of focusing on print and electronic resources, this event addresses first-year students' affective feelings about using the library. The library, decorated in a colorful party theme, uses fun activities to break down the barriers between students and library staff, encouraging students to return to the library when research help is needed (Cahoy and Bichel 2004).

During the two-day Luau visitors "might find students creating balloon animals with library staff, trying their luck at a Stock Market Treasure Hunt Game, bowling with coconuts or trying to outrace a library administrator in an 'Aloha Sack Race'" (Cahoy and Bichel 2004, 50). The main purpose of the Luau is to focus on fun, play, and personal interaction to help reduce students' fear of the library (Cahoy and Bichel 2004, 50).

A Librarian for Freshmen

To help freshmen students at Bowling Green State University (BGSU) overcome their library anxiety and become more proficient using its resources, the library designed a new position dubbed the "first-year experience" librarian (Davis 1999). This position provides library instruction and tours to the Success courses, which are designed to help freshmen make a successful transition from high school to college. Librarians at BGSU discovered that the personal touch provided by the "first-year experience" librarian was important and, in fact, helped bring students back repeatedly.

Humor in the Classroom

In a 2006 article, Billie Walker demonstrated that librarians can use humor in bibliographic sessions. What better way, he argued, to reduce library anxiety than by introducing humor. Librarian can use humor as a teaching tool to help reduce anxiety, promote classroom participation, and help students get more comfortable with their library's resources and services. Walker provided much practical help to the instruction librarian who hopes to infuse some humor into the classroom. He also dispels the fact that you do not need to be a comedian to use humor effectively.

Education through Entertainment

Western Michigan University Library staff created and hosted "an evening of instructional games to provide experiential learning, social interactions, and fun in the library for scholarship-seeking Millennials. Students discovered information in archival materials, compared search results in a library database and Google, examined plagiarism issues, formatted citations, and used the catalog to locate specific items throughout the library" (Behr, Bundza, and Cockrell 2007, 2). This event helped to build positive relationships between students and the library staff, which helped to reduce library anxiety in all students.

Creative Videos

At Brigham Young University in Provo, Utah librarians created a video to help teach library research to freshmen. The video "combines special filming techniques and music to dramatize the library research experiences of two college students" (Tidwell 1994, 187). The video follows Jason and Corinne as they begin their research in English composition class. Jason is the terrified student who actually turns and runs out of the library, only to bump into Corinne who has her topic and plans for her paper in perfect order. Corinne assists Jason in the research process, moving methodically from one step to the next in order to help Jason face his fears and anxieties about libraries and research. The video was considered motivational by students and faculty alike. "Many students, overwhelmed when first doing research in the university library were able to immediately relate to Jason's phobic images" (Tidwell 1994, 190). This video not only validated the anxiety that students experienced, it also provided a practical approach to combat that anxiety.

Roving Reference

Many students are hesitant to approach the reference librarian to ask for research or reference assistance. At Diablo Valley College in California, the roving reference librarian helps to create a more approachable atmosphere. As library resources become more varied, it becomes more important to provide library instruction that will enhance the research skills of patrons. Students, at first did not approach the roving librarian; however, when a more proactive approach was taken, patrons accepted the offer of help. The roving librarian provides several benefits to patrons (Ramirez 1994, 356).

1. Roving to provide assistance to patrons sends a signal to patrons that it is OK to not know how to use the resources and seek the help of a professional.

2. Patrons are assisted at the point of need and they do not have to abandon their workstations in order to seek help.
3. No desk separates patrons from the librarian. This close proximity helps to break down communication barriers.
4. The patron has the opportunity to learn through a hands-on approach; the Rover instructs patrons in the use of the equipment and resources.
5. The one-on-one approach provides more individualized attention, which helps alleviate anxiety.

Interventions that help students feel more relaxed and less intimidated when entering the library will serve as a catalyst for the development of library and information literacy. These programs and services mentioned above serve to break down those initial barriers that exist in libraries and to reduce library anxiety. Once initial barriers are removed librarians reach students with formal instruction to introduce them to the wonderful world of research.

6 A Library Anxiety Research Agenda for the Future

Library anxiety has been a subject of research for over two decades now, yet there is more research to be done. We would be remiss if we neglected to encourage further research, particularly as it relates to our endeavors and knowledge of the matter. In this chapter we will attempt to highlight possible areas for further research.

The current survey instrument used to measure library anxiety, the Library Anxiety Scale, was originally developed and validated by Sharon Bostick in 1992. While this survey has proven to be an excellent tool, library anxiety research would benefit from an updated survey. As discussed previously, the survey devotes only three questions to mechanical barriers, and these questions revolve around photocopiers and change machines. Given when the survey was developed, it is hardly surprising that little if any attention was devoted to such technology as computers, databases, and electronic resources. Development and validation of an updated library anxiety scale reflecting the current state of libraries would greatly benefit future library anxiety research.

Broadly stated, the study of library anxiety could benefit from further research into reducing library anxiety. Much research to date relates to understanding library anxiety in terms of who it effects and how it effects them and proving that it is a real and harmful phenomenon. Aside from this project, however, little work has focused on identifying the best approaches to treating and reducing library anxiety. We highly encourage others to continue this research and foster an understanding of these methods for reducing library anxiety and comforting students.

More specifically, this research project was unavoidably limited in nature, as it involved students at a single university using a single online tutorial. In order to provide comparison data, it would be beneficial to see similar studies done on other campuses. Such research would involve different students, different libraries, different library staff, and different online tutorials. It would be beneficial to determine if the experience and findings of this study are unique to Slippery Rock University or if they apply at other schools.

In addition to encouraging similar studies, we also encourage research that considers variables beyond those we used. This study was limited to freshmen; the statistical variables concentrated on gender, major, and number of library visits. The difference in effectiveness of treatment between traditional and non-traditional students, American and international students, and various ethnicities are just a few examples of variables that might further efforts to reduce library anxiety and understand methods of treatment.

Lastly, we suggest the possibility of testing different treatment methods from those we tested or testing the same treatment methods in combination. Our study was limited to these methods that we believed to be the most common in libraries across the country. Other treatment methods should be tested. The research team questioned, for example, the feasibility of combining some of the treatment methods tested. In other words, combine classroom instruction and an online tutorial by exposing a group of students to both. Would this combination of interventions prove more beneficial to students, particularly those with high levels of anxiety?

The future of library anxiety research offers many possibilities and opportunities to enhance the relationship between libraries and students. It is a fascinating field of research and as more and more information is discovered, librarians and libraries will better equipped to address the informational needs of the next generations. We encourage further research and welcome any questions or conversations.

Conclusion

It has been well documented that library anxiety affects many college students, regardless of background or a tendency toward trait anxiety. It is also well documented that the consequences of this anxiety range from academic procrastination to incomplete theses and dissertations. The causes for library anxiety are treatable and most often stem from an insecure and overwhelming feeling or a simple lack of understanding. As such, library anxiety in academic institutions can and should be treated.

Librarians, particularly academic librarians, have long been providing user instruction, teaching students how to find, evaluate, and use information responsibly. Since its inception, library instruction has included both classroom instruction and individual point-of-need assistance. More recently, computer assisted instruction (CAI) has become an alternate venue for delivering library instruction. Regardless of delivery style, the point of instruction has always been to assist students in using the library and information.

It seems natural then for instruction to be a consideration in alleviating library anxiety. The question, however, that prompted this study is whether one form of instruction is better at reducing library anxiety then another. The research team was not concerned with increased library skills, but rather the reduction of library anxiety. The team found that group instruction in a classroom setting and an online tutorial most effectively reduced library anxiety in freshmen students when compared to one-on-one instruction and no instruction.

Library anxiety, however, does not have to be treated through instruction alone. Countless libraries across the country have initiated innovative programs that help combat anxiety and ease freshmen into academic libraries. The simple act of reaching out, acknowledging the uncomfortable feeling, reassuring students, and demonstrating a kind and user-friendly environment, regardless of delivery method, can go a long way in reducing library anxiety. The important thing is to be proactive and to take responsibility for not only ensuring that students use the library and information well, but also that they use it without fear. Academic libraries have as much a responsibility to ease library anxiety as they do to ensure that information is being used responsibly. After all, without being comfortable using information, using it responsibly is putting the cart before the horse.

Appendix A: Methodology and the Ordered Logit Model

Implementing an OLM to the Study of Library Anxiety

In this section, we show how the Ordered Logit Model was used to estimate the effectiveness of treatments for library anxiety using the 2007 sample as an example. This exposition also allows us to introduce variable names and mnemonics necessary for the reader to understand the tables of results included in appendix B.

As explained in previous sections, at the heart of the OLM is the explicit assumption that a latent variable y^* (a covariant with library anxiety) ranging from $-\infty$ to ∞ is mapped to the responses y obtained from the students sampled. The students' responses y, however, have to be ordered in the same direction in which we expect anxiety levels to increase. We must, therefore, attach values to the ordered choices 'strongly disagree' (SD), 'disagree' (D), 'uncertain' (U), 'agree' (A), and 'strongly agree' (SA). The absolute values of the numbers used are irrelevant so long as higher numbers are associated with choices representing higher levels of anxiety. We chose the numbers one through five, even though any other set of increasing numbers would have worked just as well. Care had to be exercised, however, because some questions expressed negative sentiments regarding some aspect of library use. For these questions, the value '1' should be attached to the choice (SD) and the value '5' to the choice (SA). For questions that posited positive sentiments regarding the use of the library, the reverse mapping would be called for.

The mapping between the observed y values and the latent values y^* is of course not a one to one mapping. A range of values of the latent variable y^* would be expected to map to just one value of the observed variable y. Graphically, we would expect the relationship between y^* and y to be as follows for negative questions:

Figure A.1.

$-\infty$	τ_1	τ_2	τ_3	τ_4
1	2	3	4	5
(SD)	(D)	(U)	(A)	(SA)

Where the τ's are values marking the thresholds or cutoff points where the student becomes more likely to change his or her response. Only four cutoff points are needed to differentiate between five different choices. For questions reflecting positively on some aspect of library use, the mapping would look as follows:

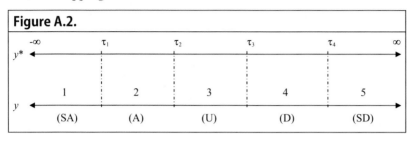

Figure A.2.

The latent function y^* we constructed as follows:

$$[1] \quad y_i^* = \beta_0 + \beta_1(g1*t) + \beta_2(g2*t) + \beta_3(g3*t) + \beta_4(g4*t)$$
$$+ \beta_5(gender) + \beta_6(libvisits) + \beta_7(major) + \varepsilon_i$$

where 'i' stands for individual i = 1,…,71 and where:

g1 = 1 if student was part of treatment group 1 (Online tutoring),
   = 0 otherwise
g2 = 1 if student was part of treatment group 2 (Control group),
   = 0 otherwise
g3 = 1 if student was part of treatment group 3 (One-on-One instruction), = 0 otherwise
g4 = 1 if student was part of treatment group 4 (Group instruction), = 0 otherwise
t = 0 observation obtained during the pre-treatment survey (=1 during post-survey)
gender = the respondent's gender (1=female, 2=male)
libvisits = number of library visits per year (1= 0 to 2, 2= 2 to 5, & 3 = more than 5)
major = student's major (1= business, 2 = non-business)
ε_i = random error when modeling individual i.

The (g1*t) through (g4*t) variables will equal 1 only for responses during the post-treatment phase of the sampling. The coefficients estimated for these variables will then capture the effects of the treatment on each of the four treatment groups. Table B.1 in appendix B shows the maximum likelihood estimates of the coefficients for all seven independent variables and all four cutoff points for each of the forty-three questions along with their corresponding p-values.[10]

Empirical Results from Our 2007 Sample

The OLM estimates the probability that an individual selects every possible choice on every one of the forty-three questions students were supposed to answer. We decided to label the Likert scale choices as follows to make them more intuitive as we encounter them:

N = negative level anxiety
Z = zero level anxiety
L = Low level anxiety
M = medium level anxiety
H = high level anxiety

These labels were chosen simply because someone answering 'disagree' (value = 2) to a question that reflects negatively on some aspect of library use can be thought of as having zero anxiety. Answering 'strongly disagree' (value = 1) can be thought of as having negative anxiety; answering 'uncertain' (value = 3) can be thought of as having 'low' level anxiety; answering 'agree' (value = 4) as having 'medium' level anxiety, and answering 'strongly agree' (value = 5) as having 'high' level anxiety. A summary of the choices, values, and labels for both negative and positive questions would appear as follows:

Table A.1. Positive and Negative Questions: Labels & Values Chosen					
Negative Questions			**Positive Questions**		
Choice	Value	Label	Choice	Value	Label
SD	1	N	SA	1	N
D	2	Z	A	2	Z
U	3	L	U	3	L
A	4	M	D	4	M
SA	5	H	SD	5	H

10. Goodness of fit tests were performed on a fully-specified model such as that in equation [1] and on equations omitting the variable 'major' which was most often found to not be statistically significant. The information criteria statistic BIC which weights the pros and cons of including a variable as an explanatory variable lent support to the inclusion of the variable 'major' in all forty-three equations. Support for its inclusion ranged from 'weak' to 'positive' to 'strong' and to 'very strong', but its inclusion was supported nonetheless.

In this study, we evaluate treatment effectiveness for all questions as a whole, and for subsets of questions that define different dimensions of library use. Table A.2 identifies these different dimensions and the questions from the Library Anxiety Scale that belong to each dimension.

Table A.2. Library-Use Dimensions		
Dimension Label	Dimension Name	Question Number of Questions included
All	Overall Anxiety	1 through 43
D1	Barriers with Staff	3 thru 8, 12, 14, 15, 21, 22, 27, 33, 34, 39
D2	Affective Barriers	1, 2, 9, 11, 16, 17, 24, 37, 38, 42, 43
D3	Comfort with the Library	18, 19, 20, 23, 25, 26, 31, 32
D4	Knowledge of the Library	13, 28, 29, 35, 41
D5	Mechanical Barriers	30, 36, 40

Operational Definitions of Treatment Effectiveness

Estimation of the model produced a 142 by 215 matrix of probabilities. The number of rows 142 represents 71 students being sampled twice: once during pre-treatment and once during post-treatment. The number of columns represents five estimated probabilities for each of forty-three questions.[11] The model thus computes a total of 430 probabilities for each student, 215 for his/her responses during the pre-treatment and 215 for his/her responses during the post-treatment phases of the study. Treatment effectiveness has to be defined as a function of all these probabilities. How we achieved this is explained in this section.

To ease exposition, a shorthand mnemonic for these probabilities is needed. We shall write $p_j q_k(0)$ to refer to the estimated probability

---

11.   For some questions (usually two or three out of forty-three), the model estimated only three cutoff points. This meant that no student chose a particular anxiety level choice for those questions so there was no information available to estimate a cutoff point. Care had to be exercised to make sure the choice not selected was clearly identified. In all cases, the choice never selected by anyone was usually an extreme choice such as either SA or SD. When this happened the matrix of estimated probabilities would of course not have 215 columns.

an individual selects choice j = N, Z, L, M, H on question k = 1, …,43 during the pre-treatment phase of the survey. The shorthand $p_j q_k(1)$ would refer to the same probability but during the post-treatment phase of the study. We start by defining the following probabilities:

$p_j q_{ALL}(0)$ = probability a certain individual selects choice j = N, Z, L, M, H when all questions are considered during the pre-treatment phase of the study.

$p_j q_{ALL}(1)$ = probability a certain individual selects choice j = N, Z, L, M, H when all questions are considered during the post-treatment phase of the study.

We decided to make the overall probability of selecting choice j, say j = N, the average of selecting choice 'N' an all 43 questions. Thus in general:

$$p_j q_{ALL}(0) = \frac{1}{43}\left[\sum_{k=1}^{43} p_j q_k(0)\right] \text{ for j = N, Z, L, M, H}$$

And

$$p_j q_{ALL}(1) = \frac{1}{43}\left[\sum_{k=1}^{43} p_j q_k(1)\right] \text{ for j = N, Z, L, M, H}$$

The laws of probability require that on a particular question the probability a student selects any choice (either N, or Z, or L, or M, or H) must equal 1. In other words:

$$[2] \quad \sum_{j=N,Z,L,M,H} p_j q_k(t) = 1$$

for any question k=1,…,43 during either pre (t=0) or post treatment (t=1).

Equation [2] will ensure that the probability a student selects any choice (either N, or Z, or L, or M, or H) when all questions are considered will also equal 1. In other words:

$$[3] \quad \sum_{j=N,Z,L,M,H} p_j q_{ALL}(t) = 1$$

during either t = 0 or t=1.

More explicitly:

$$[4] \quad p_N q_{ALL}(0) + p_Z q_{ALL}(0) + p_L q_{ALL}(0) + p_M q_{ALL}(0) + p_H q_{ALL}(0) = 1$$

And

[5] $p_N q_{ALL}(1) + p_Z q_{ALL}(1) + p_L q_{ALL}(1) + p_M q_{ALL}(1) + p_H q_{ALL}(1) = 1$

For a student, a reduction in anxiety should be reflected in increases in the probabilities of selecting choice N (negative anxiety) and/or of selecting choice Z (zero anxiety) when post-treatment choices are compared to pre-treatment choices. We therefore define a student's degree of anxiety reduction (AR) as the change in the overall probability the student selects choice N plus the overall change in the probability the student selects choice Z. Formally:

[6] $AR_{ALL} = [p_N q_{ALL}(1) - p_N q_{ALL}(0)] + [p_Z q_{ALL}(1) - p_Z q_{ALL}(0)]$

To make exposition easier to follow, we introduce another shorthand definition.

Let $\Delta p_j q_{ALL} = p_j q_{ALL}(1) - p_j q_{ALL}(0)$ for any j = N, Z, L, M, H
This allows us to rewrite equation [6] as:

[7] $AR_{ALL} = \Delta p_N q_{ALL} + \Delta p_Z q_{ALL}$

Notice that since equations [4] and [5] are equal, subtracting equation [4] from equation [5] should equal zero. This subtraction can be written as follows:

[8] $\Delta p_N q_{ALL} + \Delta p_Z q_{ALL} + \Delta p_L q_{ALL} + \Delta p_M q_{ALL} + \Delta p_H q_{ALL} = 0$

Substituting equation [7] on equation [8] allows us to write:

[9] $AR_{ALL} + \Delta p_L q_{ALL} + \Delta p_M q_{ALL} + \Delta p_H q_{ALL} = 0$

Or,

[10] $AR_{ALL} = - [\Delta p_L q_{ALL} + \Delta p_M q_{ALL} + \Delta p_H q_{ALL}]$

Equations [7] and [10] suggest there are two ways of measuring the degree of anxiety reduction (AR) for any given student as a result of a treatment. Equation [7] is computationally easier and is the formulation we used to compute the change in the probability of reducing anxiety.

Equation [7] measures anxiety reduction as the sum of net changes in the probabilities a student selects choices 'N' and 'Z' while equation [10] equates anxiety reduction to the negative of the sum of net changes in the probabilities the student selects choices 'L', 'M, and 'H'. Both ways should be equivalent as increases in the probabilities of selecting lower anxiety choices (N and Z) will have to come at the expense of reduced probabilities of selecting greater anxiety choices (L and M and H). Equation [10] can be used to illustrate three possible cases:

Case 1: The changes in each of the probabilities of selecting choices 'L', 'M' and 'Z' are all negative. That is $\Delta p_L q_{ALL}$, $\Delta p_M q_{ALL}$ and $\Delta p_H q_{ALL}$ all show reductions in the probabilities of selecting choices that reflect anxiety. The negative sign in equation [10] makes anxiety reduction (AR) positive and the student exhibits a significant reduction in anxiety as a result of the treatment.

Case 2: The changes in each of the probabilities of selecting choices 'L', 'M' and 'Z' are all positive. That is $\Delta p_L q_{ALL}$, $\Delta p_M q_{ALL}$ and $\Delta p_H q_{ALL}$ all show increases in the probabilities of selecting choices that reflect anxiety. The negative sign in equation [10] makes anxiety reduction (AR) negative and the student exhibits a significant increase in anxiety as a result of the treatment.

Case 3: The changes in some of the probabilities of selecting choices 'L', 'M' and 'Z' are positive, while others are negative. In this case, the sum of the terms $\Delta p_L q_{ALL}$, $\Delta p_M q_{ALL}$ and $\Delta p_H q_{ALL}$ will be smaller in absolute value than in cases 1 and 2, and their sum may be negative, positive or even zero. In this case individual changes in these terms are not as important as the value of the overall sum. If the sum is negative, the student will have experienced a net reduction in anxiety and if positive, a net increase in anxiety as a result of the treatment. A sum equal to zero indicates no net increase or decrease in the overall level of anxiety.

The analysis of the treatments' effectiveness on different dimensions of library use as these were defined on table A.2 proceeds the same way as the procedure just outlined. The subscript "ALL" on the variable 'q' is simply replaced on equations [3] through [10] with the appropriate mnemonic 'D1' or 'D2' or 'D3' or 'D4' or 'D5'.

Estimating Treatment Effectiveness

Our statistical methodology as outlined thus far produces estimates of the change in the probability of reducing anxiety (AR) caused by a treatment on each of the students sampled. This AR variable together with identifying information such as the student's gender, the student's major, his treatment group (group), and the student's number of library visits per year (libvisits) forms a seventy-one by five reduced matrix of information that we now use to make inferences on treatment effectiveness. Whatever inferential tool we use, it must separate the effect of the treatment from such influences as the student's gender, major, and number of library visits a year. Given that our independent variables are all categorical variables, the choice of an analysis of variance technique (ANOVA) seemed like a logical choice.

Appendix C shows the results obtained from using ANOVA first on all questions as a whole, and then on the analysis of the five different dimensions of library use as these were outlined on table A.2.

Introduction to the Ordered Logit Model

In this section we provide a relatively brief introduction to the Ordered Logit Model (OLM) and how it estimates the probability that an individual will respond to a certain question in some particular way. For a more thorough treatment of the Ordered Logit Model we recommend J. Scott Long's "Regression Models for Categorical and Limited Dependent Variables" (1997) and J. Scott Long and Jeremy Freese "Regression Models for Categorical Dependent Variables Using Stata" (2006).

The OLM was designed to make inferences using ordinal level data. In this study our data represent how students felt about different aspects of using our library. Though the response choices can be clearly arranged in some order, deciding which one comes first and which one goes last is not always apparent. The 'proper' order of the response choices is a function of what the investigator is attempting to measure. Suppose, for example, the alternatives strongly disagree (SD), disagree (D), uncertain (U), agree (A), and strongly agree (SA) are offered as response choices to the statement: "The people who work at the circulation desk are helpful." An increasing level of anxiety would be reflected in ordering the choices as SA, A, U, D, SD. If, however, the level of satisfaction with use of the library is what is of interest, then the opposite ordering would be called for. It is indeed possible, then, that if the intensity of how individuals feel about some statement is what is of interest, the proper ordering of the choices might run from SA or SD to A or D to U.

A Latent Variable Interpretation of the Ordered Logit Model

An attractive property of the OLM is its ability to relate discrete observations on some variable 'y' to an unobserved but presumed latent variable y^*. Observations on 'y' are thought of as incomplete empirical evidence of the underlying existence of y^*. These two variables are assumed to be related as follows (see figures A.1 and A.2):

$$y_i = m \text{ if } \tau_{m-1} \leq y_i^* \leq \tau_m \text{ for m=1 to J}$$

The $\tau's$ are referred to as thresholds or cutoff points. The latent variable y^* is assumed to range from $-\infty$ to ∞ which forces the cutoff points on both ends to be limitless also, that is:

$$y_i = 1 \text{ if } -\infty \leq y_i^* \leq \tau_1 \quad \text{and} \quad y_i = J \text{ if } \tau_{J-1} \leq y_i^* \leq \infty$$

The students sampled were offered five ways to respond to a statement on some dimension of library use. The value $y=1$ was equated with the lowest level of anxiety and the value $y=5$ with the highest level of anxiety. With five values for 'y' only four cutoff points need be identified. The correspondence between 'y' and y^* is as follows:

$$y_i = 1 \text{ if } -\infty \leq y_i^* \leq \tau_1$$
$$y_i = 2 \text{ if } \tau_1 \leq y_i^* \leq \tau_2$$
$$y_i = 3 \text{ if } \tau_2 \leq y_i^* \leq \tau_3$$
$$y_i = 4 \text{ if } \tau_3 \leq y_i^* \leq \tau_4$$
$$y_i = 5 \text{ if } \tau_4 \leq y_i^* \leq \infty$$

Figure A.3 illustrates how values of y^* are related to the observed values 'y' for a set of possible cutoff points τ_1 through τ_4.

Figure A.3.

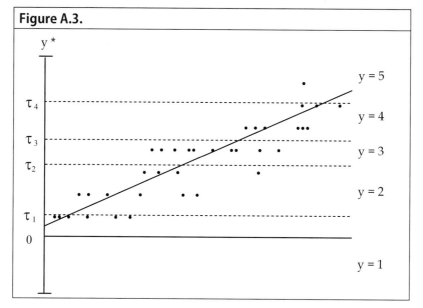

Theoretically, changes in library anxiety are reflected in the changes taking place in our latent variable y_i^*. The latter we define as follows:

[1] $y_i^* = \alpha + \beta X_i + \varepsilon_i$

The information matrix X_i is made up of identifying variables particular to individual 'i' that predispose him or her to react to a given statement in some particular way.[12]

As illustrated, suppose we had only one identifying variable x_i. Figure A.4 shows what could happen at three different values of the independent variable x_i.

Figure A.4.

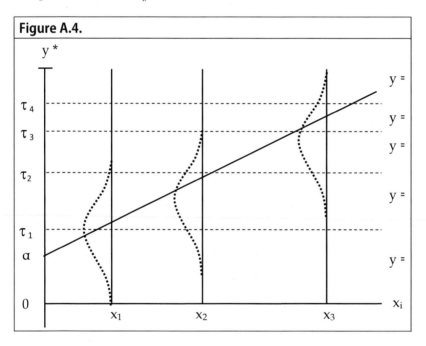

For a given pair of values α and β in equation [1] the probability we observe value $y=m$ ($m=1,\ldots,5$) is:

$$Pr(y_i = m / x_i) = Pr(\tau_{m-1} \leq y_i^* \leq \tau_m / x_i)$$

[2] *Or*

$$Pr(y_i = m / x_i) = Pr(\tau_{m-1} \leq \alpha + \beta x_i + \varepsilon_i \leq \tau_m / x_i)$$

12.   In our study the personal identifying variables we obtained from our students were: gender, average number of library visits per year (libvisits), and major.

Since the cutoff points $(\tau's)$ and the latent values y^* are simultaneously determined (see figures A.1 and A.2) equation [2] shows that the model is indeterminate up to a constant. That is to say, the same probabilities are obtained by adding a constant δ to all cutoff points and to all y^*s. In other words:

$$[3] \quad \Pr(y_i = m / x_i) = \Pr(\tau_{m-1} \le \alpha + \beta x_i + \varepsilon_i \le \tau_m / x_i)$$
$$= \Pr(\tau_{m-1} + \delta \le (\alpha + \delta) + \beta x_i + \varepsilon_i \le \tau_m + \delta / x_i)$$

Graphically equation [3] would like just as figure A.1 only that the line $(\alpha + \beta x_i)$ and the cutoff points have all been shifted by some constant δ.

The model can be identified either by anchoring the estimated line $(\alpha + \beta x_i)$ at some intercept value such as $\alpha = 0$ or by anchoring one of the cutoff points at some level such as would occur if we set $\tau_1 = 0$. Either parameterization will yield the same results. In other words, the estimated probabilities of the observed ys will be the same regardless of which parameterization is used. The statistical software Stata, which we used to estimate the Ordered Logit Model, chooses to set the intercept α to zero. This is why an intercept coefficient does not appear on the tables of estimated coefficients in appendix B.

Estimating the Probabilities of Selecting an Ordered Choice
Using Stata's parameterization we now rewrite equation [2] as:

$$\Pr(y_i = m / x_i) = \Pr(\tau_{m-1} \le \beta x_i + \varepsilon_i \le \tau_m / x_i) \quad \text{m=1 thru 5}$$
[4] Or,
$$\Pr(y_i = m / x_i) = \Pr(\tau_{m-1} - \beta x_i \le \varepsilon_i \le \tau_m - \beta x_i / x_i)$$

The probability a random variable is between two values is equal to the difference of the cumulative density function evaluated at those two values. Mathematically:

$$[5] \quad \Pr(y_i = m / x_i) = \Pr(\varepsilon_i \le \tau_m - \beta x_i / x_i) - \Pr(\varepsilon_i \le \tau_{m-1} - \beta x_i / x_i)$$
$$= F(\tau_m - \beta x_i) - F(\tau_{m-1} - \beta x_i)$$

where F stands for the cumulative density function of the random variable ε_i.

We can now define the probabilities for all y_i values as follows:

$$\Pr(y_i = 1/x_i) = F(\tau_1 - \beta x_i) - F(-\infty - \beta x_i) = F(\tau_1 - \beta x_i)$$
$$\Pr(y_i = 2/x_i) = F(\tau_2 - \beta x_i) - F(\tau_1 - \beta x_i)$$
$$\Pr(y_i = 3/x_i) = F(\tau_3 - \beta x_i) - F(\tau_2 - \beta x_i)$$
$$\Pr(y_i = 4/x_i) = F(\tau_4 - \beta x_i) - F(\tau_3 - \beta x_i)$$
$$\Pr(y_i = 5/x_i) = F(\infty - \beta x_i) - F(\tau_4 - \beta x_i) = 1 - F(\tau_4 - \beta x_i)$$

Distributional Assumptions

The probability equations as stated above require that we assume a probability distribution for the error term ε_i. The two most widely used distributions for ε_i are the Normal distribution and the Logistic distribution. Assuming ε_i follows a Normal distribution leads to the Ordered Probit Model (OPM) while assuming it follows a Logistic distribution leads to the Ordered Logit Model (OLM), which is the assumption we used to estimate our probabilities. The cumulative density function of the Logistic distribution for some value ε_i is written as follows:

[6] $F(\varepsilon_i) = \dfrac{\exp(\varepsilon_i)}{1 + \exp(\varepsilon_i)}$

Estimation

Assuming that what an individual selects for an answer is independent of what others chose as their answers, the probability of observing all choices as they were actually observed can then be written as follows:

[7] $L(\beta, \tau / \text{ y, X}) = \prod\limits_{i=1}^{N} p_{i,m}$

where $p_{i,m}$ is the probability individual 'i' selects choice $y=m$ which is the choice the individual actually selected. These probabilities are as described in equation [5] using the logistic cumulative function of equation [6]. The resulting so-called likelihood function is a function of the cutoff values and the slope β coefficients for given values of y as observed and the information matrix X.

The estimated cutoff points $(\tau's)$ and slope coefficients (β's) are the values for these coefficients, which maximize the likelihood function L as defined by equation [7]. These coefficients are much easier to find by maximizing the log of the likelihood function, which is written as follows:

$$[8] \quad Ln(L) = \sum_{m=1}^{5} \sum_{y_i=m} Ln[F(\tau_m - X\beta) - F(\tau_{m-1} - X\beta)]$$

the summation $\displaystyle\sum_{y_i=m}$ indicates summing over all individuals which selected choice $y=m$.

Maximization of equation [8] is done using numerical algorithms such as the Newton-Raphson method of steepest ascent. Maddala (1983, 48-49) shows that the Newton-Raphson estimates of τ and β lead to a global maximum and that these estimates are consistent, asymptotically normal, and asymptotically efficient.

Appendix B:
Coefficient Tables

Table B.1. Estimated Coefficient by Statement using OLM – 2007 Results

State-ment	g1*t	g2*t	g3*t	g4*t	Gender	Library Visits	Major	cut1	cut2	cut3	cut4
1	-0.053	-0.391	-1.213	-0.729	-0.474	0.236	0.578	0.621	2.263	2.893	4.998
	0.8281	0.2051	0.0000	0.0000	0.0946	0.0235	0.2585	0.3979	0.0014	0.0000	0.0000
2	-1.042	-1.065	-1.466	-1.390	-0.026	0.618	0.550	0.300	2.610	3.636	6.883
	0.0026	0.0000	0.0000	0.0000	0.9097	0.0028	0.1197	0.7457	0.0063	0.0010	0.0000
3	-0.706	0.606	-0.517	-0.549	-0.086	-0.197	0.002	-1.668	0.121	2.164	4.423
	0.1758	0.2938	0.0779	0.0214	0.9079	0.2276	0.9971	0.0439	0.8886	0.0569	0.0007
4	-0.775	0.363	-1.466	-1.160	-0.542	-0.213	0.126	-2.439	-0.536	1.951	2.914
	0.0733	0.2616	0.0000	0.0000	0.3413	0.0000	0.0235	0.0000	0.0024	0.0000	0.0000
5	-0.759	0.091	-1.468	-0.196	-0.338	-0.230	0.148	-1.766	-0.240	2.815	3.749
	0.0740	0.7983	0.0000	0.1193	0.7021	0.9050	0.7120	0.0887	0.7901	0.0000	0.0000
6	-0.647	0.178	-0.826	-0.661	-0.130	-0.172	0.489	-1.332	0.686	2.716	-
	0.1316	0.6632	0.0002	0.0014	0.8525	0.4980	0.3109	0.0001	0.1025	0.0000	-
7	-0.494	0.436	-0.993	-0.108	-0.534	-0.045	0.301	-1.400	0.577	3.321	5.138
	0.4129	0.4615	0.0000	0.6573	0.6239	0.8544	0.4958	0.0079	0.1395	0.0000	0.0000
8	-0.496	0.455	-1.197	-0.498	-0.724	-0.057	0.488	1.381	0.491	3.202	5.321
	0.2837	0.1922	0.0000	0.0000	0.2852	0.7649	0.2661	0.0069	0.2386	0.0000	0.0000
9	-0.556	0.363	-1.383	-0.663	-0.719	0.299	0.197	-1.591	0.452	1.128	3.277
	0.0960	0.0059	0.0000	0.0000	0.3704	0.1827	0.6745	0.2902	0.7568	0.4551	0.0258
10	-0.705	-0.879	-1.259	-0.147	-1.074	0.092	0.146	-2.442	-0.604	0.196	2.206
	0.0256	0.0555	0.0001	0.6019	0.0455	0.6974	0.5712	0.1054	0.5909	0.8461	0.0015
11	-0.902	0.476	-1.376	-0.298	-0.783	0.073	0.379	-1.910	-0.164	0.965	2.922
	0.0484	0.0875	0.0000	0.2357	0.3210	0.6579	0.3022	0.0284	0.8798	0.3527	0.0002
12	-0.450	0.235	-2.040	-0.743	-0.458	-0.177	0.100	-2.530	-0.381	2.275	3.701
	0.2663	0.1901	0.0000	0.0000	0.3965	0.0346	0.7127	0.0003	0.3472	0.0000	0.0000
13	-1.121	-0.294	-0.253	-0.168	0.187	-0.436	-0.466	-3.982	-1.484	-0.390	1.206
	0.0000	0.1826	0.4178	0.4308	0.8456	0.0578	0.1533	0.0000	0.0368	0.6466	0.1777
14	-0.137	0.538	-0.063	0.330	-0.315	-0.356	0.475	-1.888	0.844	2.230	3.219
	0.5685	0.0266	0.8874	0.3481	0.4876	0.1391	0.5322	0.0068	0.2853	0.0001	0.0000
15	0.180	0.820	-1.027	-0.132	-0.648	-0.363	0.552	-1.869	0.180	2.880	5.013
	0.5349	0.0000	0.0000	0.3715	0.2514	0.0352	0.0059	0.0000	0.5019	0.0000	0.0000

Table B.1. Estimated Coefficient by Statement using OLM – 2007 Results

State-ment	g1*t	g2*t	g3*t	g4*t	Gender	Library Visits	Major	cut1	cut2	cut3	cut4
16	-0.160	0.478	-1.065	-0.022	-0.817	-0.129	0.244	-2.108	0.274	1.359	3.209
	0.4186	0.2161	0.0000	0.9149	0.0612	0.5587	0.6890	0.0547	0.7959	0.1297	0.0003
17	-0.630	0.168	-0.445	-0.086	-0.610	-0.154	0.412	-1.564	-0.038	1.116	2.737
	0.0066	0.6244	0.0581	0.7052	0.3657	0.4749	0.2196	0.2518	0.9767	0.4258	0.0022
18	-0.333	-0.256	-0.070	-0.192	0.224	-0.556	0.014	-2.160	0.372	2.038	2.758
	0.3009	0.5452	0.6767	0.2691	0.6963	0.0364	0.9889	0.1992	0.8249	0.1079	0.0146
19	-0.720	-0.226	-0.582	-0.783	-0.429	-0.550	0.267	-2.451	0.229	1.294	1.822
	0.1015	0.2812	0.0094	0.0000	0.3410	0.0242	0.7266	0.0350	0.8551	0.2833	0.0745
20	-0.506	0.908	-1.101	-0.294	-0.809	-0.422	0.536	-2.019	-0.303	2.788	4.068
	0.0272	0.0000	0.0000	0.0000	0.1343	0.0373	0.0178	0.0037	0.6210	0.0000	0.0000
21	0.365	0.948	-0.361	-0.307	-0.310	-0.364	-0.018	-2.429	0.390	1.533	3.102
	0.1474	0.0262	0.2554	0.3484	0.5300	0.0091	0.9544	0.0010	0.4461	0.0015	0.0000
22	-1.339	-0.763	-0.381	-0.824	-0.032	-0.590	0.005	-3.241	-0.510	0.913	1.361
	0.0000	0.0000	0.1812	0.0005	0.9411	0.0000	0.9910	0.0000	0.4413	0.0337	0.0000
23	-0.856	0.893	-1.200	-0.769	-0.084	-0.538	0.242	-2.708	-0.695	1.791	-
	0.0010	0.0057	0.0000	0.0000	0.9090	0.0051	0.5025	0.0002	0.1186	0.0001	-
24	-0.209	0.617	-0.558	0.116	-0.681	-0.356	0.060	-3.154	-0.806	1.099	2.784
	0.3201	0.0084	0.0189	0.6472	0.2824	0.0398	0.8828	0.0058	0.3406	0.2326	0.0236
25	-0.224	-0.622	-0.555	-0.177	0.284	-0.380	0.111	-1.119	0.388	2.908	3.207
	0.5321	0.0638	0.0000	0.1426	0.5578	0.1943	0.8713	0.2060	0.6331	0.0001	0.0000
26	-0.542	0.450	-1.107	-0.839	-0.203	-0.364	1.810	-3.258	-0.779	1.635	3.590
	0.0532	0.0232	0.0000	0.0000	0.4431	0.0000	0.5542	0.0000	0.0194	0.0062	0.0000
27	-1.013	0.202	-0.301	-0.474	0.234	-0.240	0.221	-1.449	0.585	2.494	4.047
	0.0064	0.4984	0.0034	0.0007	0.6206	0.0194	0.2585	0.0003	0.0392	0.0000	0.0000
28	-0.027	-0.557	0.186	-0.161	0.214	-0.466	-0.553	-3.328	-1.143	0.368	1.301
	0.9310	0.0008	0.7165	0.6632	0.7118	1.0020	0.2754	0.0006	0.1666	0.6097	0.0853
29	0.885	0.088	1.250	0.019	0.583	-0.372	-1.038	-3.303	-0.645	0.841	2.438
	0.0000	0.7991	0.0000	0.9112	0.1239	0.0471	0.0008	0.0000	0.4185	0.3331	0.0522
30	-0.340	0.397	-0.710	-0.750	-0.711	-0.006	0.947	-2.582	-0.423	3.740	5.722
	0.5106	0.3320	0.0182	0.0234	0.1559	0.9605	0.0001	0.0189	0.5958	0.0000	0.0000
31	-0.273	-0.342	0.034	0.449	0.281	-0.125	-0.306	-3.090	-1.548	0.144	2.166
	0.0000	0.1845	0.9126	0.2068	0.5262	0.3588	0.3420	0.0005	0.0355	0.8556	0.0578
32	-0.891	-0.625	0.002	-0.379	-0.323	0.050	0.350	-2.683	-0.334	2.906	4.275
	0.0959	0.2438	0.9944	0.0391	0.7663	0.6788	0.5645	0.0366	0.8080	0.0283	0.0000
33	-0.499	0.205	-1.752	-0.358	-0.815	-0.514	0.466	-2.679	-0.343	1.877	3.654
	0.2053	0.3990	0.0000	0.0000	0.2644	0.0000	0.3411	0.0006	0.6189	0.0021	0.0000

Table B.1. Estimated Coefficient by Statement using OLM – 2007 Results

State-ment	g1*t	g2*t	g3*t	g4*t	Gender	Library Visits	Major	cut1	cut2	cut3	cut4
34	-1.201	-0.398	-0.999	-1.469	-0.140	-0.349	0.083	-3.368	-0.981	1.702	2.845
	0.0312	0.3608	0.0000	0.0000	0.8735	0.0000	0.6457	0.0000	0.0792	0.0003	0.0003
35	-0.657	-0.428	-0.402	-0.103	0.525	-0.407	-0.033	-1.636	0.511	1.976	2.707
	0.1440	0.2832	0.0242	0.5593	0.2563	0.0001	0.9360	0.0220	0.4803	0.0000	0.0000
36	-0.788	0.458	-1.328	-0.005	-0.058	0.207	1.021	-0.474	1.307	4.233	7.054
	0.0223	0.3477	0.0001	0.9867	0.9314	0.3410	0.0388	0.7742	0.2987	0.0012	0.0000
37	-1.276	0.618	-0.772	-0.415	-0.355	-0.273	0.911	-1.950	0.233	3.149	0.571
	0.0000	0.1226	0.0000	0.0081	0.6754	0.2059	0.0230	0.0473	0.7744	0.0000	0.0000
38	-1.192	0.344	-0.916	-0.246	-1.200	-0.019	0.526	-2.478	-0.268	1.052	3.402
	0.0251	0.5175	0.0000	0.1340	0.0553	0.9495	0.0621	0.0145	0.7899	0.3134	0.0054
39	-0.604	0.510	-0.869	-0.558	-0.481	-0.216	0.789	-1.260	0.978	3.340	4.886
	0.1448	0.1805	0.0000	0.0068	0.4535	0.1320	0.0011	0.0037	0.0611	0.0000	0.0000
40	-0.611	0.441	-1.698	-0.508	-0.488	-0.356	0.381	-3.696	-1.784	3.165	3.869
	0.0068	0.0795	0.0000	0.0000	0.1327	0.0075	0.4857	0.0012	0.0659	0.0001	0.0000
41	-0.428	-0.310	-0.665	-0.599	0.220	-0.594	0.044	-2.234	0.214	1.350	2.099
	0.0700	0.2294	0.0000	0.0000	0.5654	0.0003	0.9301	0.0087	0.8193	0.0572	0.0000
42	-0.667	0.088	-1.672	-0.590	-0.465	-0.316	0.689	-2.753	-1.014	3.289	5.127
	0.0023	0.6374	0.0000	0.0052	0.1663	0.1858	0.0901	0.0419	0.3351	0.0005	0.0000
43	-1.377	-0.455	-0.784	-0.359	0.571	0.369	0.520	-0.502	1.345	3.051	5.192
	0.0000	0.1526	0.0000	0.0024	0.2740	0.0774	0.0981	0.2708	0.0003	0.0000	0.0000

Table B.2. ANOVA Estimates of Group Effectiveness in Reducing Library Anxiety – 2006

2006 N=72			2006 N=54			2006 N=47		
Overall	Coefficient	P Value	Overall	Coefficient	P Value	Overall	Coefficient	P Value
Online	0.2892894	0.000	Online	.2501949	0.000	Online	.2389417	0.000
Control	0.2115850	0.000	Control	.2642045	0.000	Control	.2726091	0.000
1-on-1	0.1655499	0.000	1-on-1	.1834785	0.000	1-on-1	.1815811	0.000
Group	0.2423918	0.000	Group	.2781893	0.000	Group	.2500755	0.000
D1	Coefficient	P Value	D1	Coefficient	P Value	D1	Coefficient	P Value
Online	0.3733518	0.000	Online	.3312998	0.000	Online	.2766830	0.000
Control	0.2638997	0.000	Control	.3321962	0.000	Control	.3162261	0.000
1-on-1	0.2228257	0.000	1-on-1	.2551530	0.000	1-on-1	.2441483	0.000
Group	0.3212925	0.000	Group	.3977363	0.000	Group	.3539896	0.000
D2	Coefficient	P Value	D2	Coefficient	P Value	D2	Coefficient	P Value
Online	0.2885781	0.000	Online	.2509923	0.000	Online	.2445127	0.000
Control	0.1870113	0.000	Control	.2345504	0.000	Control	.2349709	0.000
1-on-1	0.1486049	0.000	1-on-1	.1101137	0.000	1-on-1	.0886338	0.000
Group	0.2589147	0.000	Group	.2380797	0.000	Group	.2021832	0.000
D3	Coefficient	P Value	D3	Coefficient	P Value	D3	Coefficient	P Value
Online	0.2990985	0.000	Online	.2789383	0.000	Online	.2943654	0.000
Control	0.2642585	0.000	Control	.3241114	0.000	Control	.3422254	0.000
1-on-1	0.1930749	0.000	1-on-1	.2867332	0.000	1-on-1	.2977033	0.000
Group	0.2203963	0.000	Group	.2651417	0.000	Group	.2254677	0.000
D4	Coefficient	P Value	D4	Coefficient	P Value	D4	Coefficient	P Value
Online	0.0657571	0.000	Online	.0452575	0.000	Online	.0584817	0.000
Control	0.0400931	0.000	Control	.0879078	0.000	Control	.1306899	0.000
1-on-1	0.0534685	0.000	1-on-1	.0532908	0.000	1-on-1	.0416373	0.000
Group	0.0158786	0.000	Group	.0718067	0.000	Group	.0471832	0.000
D5	Coefficient	P Value	D5	Coefficient	P Value	D5	Coefficient	P Value
Online	0.2271075	0.000	Online	.1129392	0.000	Online	.1922254	0.000
Control	0.1955861	0.000	Control	.1740600	0.000	Control	.2535358	0.000
1-on-1	0.0607632	0.000	1-on-1	.0467647	0.000	1-on-1	.1488769	0.000
Group	0.2194255	0.000	Group	.2102051	0.000	Group	.3154373	0.000

Table B.3. ANOVA Estimates of Group Effectiveness in Reducing Anxiety – 2007

2007 N=71			2007 N=53			2007 N=45		
Overall	Coefficient	P Value	Overall	Coefficient	P Value	Overall	Coefficient	P Value
Online	0.1211350	0.000	Online	.1452526	0.000	Online	.0932150	0.000
Control	-0.0310231	0.000	Control	-.0429605	0.000	Control	.0332704	0.000
1-on-1	0.1729840	0.000	1-on-1	.1777023	0.000	1-on-1	.1680343	0.000
Group	0.0826235	0.000	Group	.1262410	0.000	Group	.1287633	0.000
D1	Coefficient	P Value	D1	Coefficient	P Value	D1	Coefficient	P Value
Online	0.1160566	0.000	Online	.1220644	0.000	Online	.0726450	0.000
Control	-0.0767125	0.000	Control	-.0863324	0.000	Control	-.0072075	0.005
1-on-1	0.1940112	0.000	1-on-1	.1928811	0.000	1-on-1	.2125377	0.000
Group	0.1037403	0.000	Group	.1457320	0.000	Group	.1546868	0.000
D2	Coefficient	P Value	D2	Coefficient	P Value	D2	Coefficient	P Value
Online	0.1699651	0.000	Online	.2129147	0.000	Online	.1646268	0.000
Control	-0.0035828	0.013	Control	-.0138250	0.019	Control	.0349537	0.000
1-on-1	0.2388739	0.000	1-on-1	.2613311	0.000	1-on-1	.2180025	0.000
Group	0.0871849	0.000	Group	.1165587	0.000	Group	.1223360	0.000
D3	Coefficient	P Value	D3	Coefficient	P Value	D3	Coefficient	P Value
Online	0.1034112	0.000	Online	.1306272	0.000	Online	.0620980	0.000
Control	-0.0208106	0.000	Control	-.0079503	0.001	Control	.0689080	0.000
1-on-1	0.1122451	0.000	1-on-1	.1014633	0.000	1-on-1	.1055367	0.000
Group	0.0688638	0.000	Group	.1261158	0.000	Group	.1326662	0.000
D4	Coefficient	P Value	D4	Coefficient	P Value	D4	Coefficient	P Value
Online	0.0487929	0.000	Online	.0846255	0.000	Online	.0733727	0.000
Control	0.0569038	0.000	Control	.0241567	0.000	Control	.1146150	0.000
1-on-1	-0.0068224	0.000	1-on-1	-.0628957	0.000	1-on-1	-.0514287	0.000
Group	0.0300329	0.000	Group	.0561616	0.000	Group	.0525292	0.000
D5	Coefficient	P Value	D5	Coefficient	P Value	D5	Coefficient	P Value
Online	0.1196914	0.000	Online	.1305063	0.000	Online	.0262036	0.008
Control	-0.0860355	0.000	Control	-.1488581	0.000	Control	-.0028628	0.779
1-on-1	0.2653590	0.000	1-on-1	.3696921	0.000	1-on-1	.2757800	0.000
Group	0.0826740	0.000	Group	.1828829	0.000	Group	.1393907	0.000

Appendix C: ANOVA Results for 2007 Full Sample

**ESTIMATING TREATMENT EFFECTIVENESS REDUCING OVERALL ANXIETY
RESULTS USING ANOVA – 2007 SURVEY, FULL SAMPLE**

```
                        Number of obs =       71    R-squared      =  0.9985
                        Root MSE      = .002884    Adj R-squared =  0.9983

            Source |  Partial SS    df       MS                  F    Prob > F
        -----------+----------------------------------------------------------
             Model |  .343075966     7  .049010852            5894.01   0.0000
                   |
             group |  .216153504     3  .072051168            8664.82   0.0000
          libvisits |  .000395527     2  .000197764             23.78   0.0000
            gender |  .000020417     1  .000020417              2.46   0.1221
             major |  .000104941     1  .000104941             12.62   0.0007
                   |
          Residual |  .000523868    63  8.3154e-06
        -----------+----------------------------------------------------------
             Total |  .343599834    70  .004908569
```

```
        Source |      SS          df       MS             Number of obs =       71
    -----------+------------------------------           F(  8,     63) =13476.54
         Model | .896499036        8  .112062379          Prob > F      =  0.0000
      Residual | .000523868       63  8.3154e-06          R-squared     =  0.9994
    -----------+------------------------------           Adj R-squared =  0.9993
         Total | .897022904       71  .012634125          Root MSE      =  .00288
```

```
--------------------------------------------------------------------------------
   gain_All        Coef.    Std. Err.      t    P>|t|      [95% Conf. Interval]
--------------------------------------------------------------------------------
group
          1      .121135    .0009826   123.28   0.000      .1191714    .1230986
          2     -.0310231   .0012923   -24.01   0.000     -.0336055   -.0284406
          3      .172984    .0011489   150.56   0.000      .1706881     .17528
          4      .0826235   .0010384    79.57   0.000      .0805485    .0846985
libvisits
          1      .0056762   .0008567     6.63   0.000      .0039643    .0073881
          2      .0039244   .0008891     4.41   0.000      .0021477    .0057011
          3    (dropped)
gender
          1      .0013852    .000884     1.57   0.122     -.0003813    .0031518
          2    (dropped)
major
          1     -.0033169   .0009337    -3.55   0.001     -.0051827   -.0014511
          2    (dropped)
--------------------------------------------------------------------------------
```

**ESTIMATING TREATMENT EFFECTIVENESS REDUCING
DIMENSION 1: BARRIERS WITH STAFF ANXIETY
RESULTS USING ANOVA – 2007 SURVEY, FULL SAMPLE**

```
                    Number of obs =       71    R-squared      =  0.9936
                    Root MSE      =  .0079    Adj R-squared  =  0.9929

        Source |  Partial SS    df       MS              F      Prob > F
    -----------+----------------------------------------------------------
         Model |  .607261511     7  .086751644        1389.96     0.0000
               |
         group |  .362274407     3  .120758136        1934.82     0.0000
      libvisits |  .001713555     2  .000856777          13.73     0.0000
        gender |  .000433155     1  .000433155           6.94     0.0106
         major |  .000187689     1  .000187689           3.01     0.0878
               |
      Residual |  .00393203     63  .000062413
    -----------+----------------------------------------------------------
         Total |  .611193542    70  .008731336


        Source |      SS        df       MS              Number of obs =       71
    -----------+-------------------------------          F(  8,   63) =  2496.22
         Model |  1.24637484     8  .155796855          Prob > F      =   0.0000
      Residual |  .00393203     63  .000062413          R-squared     =   0.9969
    -----------+-------------------------------          Adj R-squared =   0.9965
         Total |  1.25030687    71  .017609956          Root MSE      =    .0079

    -------------------------------------------------------------------------------
       gain_D1 |     Coef.    Std. Err.      t     P>|t|     [95% Conf. Interval]
    -------------------------------------------------------------------------------
    group
             1 |   .1160566    .002692     43.11   0.000     .110677     .1214361
             2 |  -.0767125    .0035404   -21.67   0.000    -.0837875   -.0696375
             3 |   .1940112    .0031477    61.64   0.000     .1877211    .2003013
             4 |   .1037403    .0028448    36.47   0.000     .0980555    .1094251
    libvisits
             1 |   .0121128    .002347      5.16   0.000     .0074227    .0168028
             2 |   .0070678    .0024358     2.90   0.005     .0022002    .0119354
             3 |  (dropped)
    gender
             1 |   .0063803    .0024219     2.63   0.011     .0015405     .01122
             2 |  (dropped)
    major
             1 |  -.0044358    .002558     -1.73   0.088    -.0095475    .0006758
             2 |  (dropped)
    -------------------------------------------------------------------------------
```

ESTIMATING TREATMENT EFFECTIVENESS REDUCING
DIMENSION 2: AFFECTIVE BARRIERS ANXIETY
RESULTS USING ANOVA – 2007 SURVEY, FULL SAMPLE

```
                    Number of obs =      71   R-squared     =  0.9988
                    Root MSE      = .00311   Adj R-squared =  0.9987

         Source |  Partial SS    df       MS            F      Prob > F
    ------------+----------------------------------------------------------
          Model |  .515296723     7  .073613818      7609.58     0.0000
                |
          group |  .354216595     3  .118072198     12205.31     0.0000
       libvisits|  .002016338     2  .001008169       104.22     0.0000
         gender |  5.0592e-06     1  5.0592e-06         0.52     0.4723
          major |  .000321612     1  .000321612        33.25     0.0000
                |
       Residual |  .000609452    63  9.6738e-06
    ------------+----------------------------------------------------------
          Total |  .515906175    70  .007370088
```

```
      Source |      SS       df       MS              Number of obs =      71
    ---------+----------------------------             F(  8,    63) =17919.18
       Model | 1.38677771      8  .173347214           Prob > F      =  0.0000
    Residual |  .000609452    63  9.6738e-06           R-squared     =  0.9996
    ---------+----------------------------             Adj R-squared =  0.9995
       Total | 1.38738716     71  .019540664           Root MSE      = .00311
```

```
    --------------------------------------------------------------------------
       gain_D2 |      Coef.   Std. Err.      t    P>|t|     [95% Conf. Interval]
    -----------+--------------------------------------------------------------
    group      |
            1  |   .1699651   .0010598    160.37   0.000     .1678472    .172083
            2  |  -.0035828   .0013939     -2.57   0.013    -.0063682   -.0007974
            3  |   .2388739   .0012392    192.76   0.000     .2363975    .2413503
            4  |   .0871849    .00112      77.85   0.000     .0849468    .089423

    libvisits  |
            1  |  -.0133398   .000924     -14.44   0.000    -.0151862   -.0114933
            2  |  -.0055669   .000959      -5.81   0.000    -.0074833   -.0036506
            3  |  (dropped)
    gender     |
            1  |   .0006895   .0009535      0.72   0.472    -.0012159    .0025949
            2  |  (dropped)
    major      |
            1  |  -.0058066   .0010071     -5.77   0.000    -.0078191   -.0037942
            2  |  (dropped)
    --------------------------------------------------------------------------
```

**ESTIMATING TREATMENT EFFECTIVENESS REDUCING
DIMENSION 3: COMFORT WITH THE LIBRARY ANXIETY
RESULTS USING ANOVA – 2007 SURVEY, FULL SAMPLE**

```
                  Number of obs =      71   R-squared       =  0.9968
                  Root MSE      = .003021   Adj R-squared =   0.9965

       Source |  Partial SS   df       MS             F      Prob > F
  ------------+----------------------------------------------------------
        Model |  .180095286    7  .025727898       2818.39     0.0000
              |
        group |  .106168109    3   .03538937       3876.77     0.0000
     libvisits |  .004764581    2  .002382291        260.97     0.0000
       gender |  2.9605e-06    1  2.9605e-06          0.32     0.5711
        major |    .00007684    1    .00007684          8.42     0.0051
              |
     Residual |     .0005751   63  9.1286e-06
  ------------+----------------------------------------------------------
        Total |  .180670386   70  .002581006


       Source |     SS       df       MS             Number of obs =      71
  ------------+------------------------------         F(  8,    63) = 8012.03
        Model | .585107337    8  .073138417          Prob > F      =  0.0000
     Residual |    .0005751   63  9.1286e-06          R-squared     =  0.9990
  ------------+------------------------------         Adj R-squared =  0.9989
        Total | .585682438   71  .008249048          Root MSE      =  .00302

  ----------------------------------------------------------------------------
      gain_D3       Coef.   Std. Err.       t    P>|t|    [95% Conf. Interval]
  ----------------------------------------------------------------------------
  group
           1     .1034112   .0010295   100.44   0.000    .1013538    .1054686
           2    -.0208106    .001354   -15.37   0.000   -.0235164   -.0181048
           3     .1122451   .0012038    93.24   0.000    .1098395    .1146506
           4     .0688638    .001088    63.30   0.000    .0666897    .0710379
  libvisits
           1     .0200901   .0008976    22.38   0.000    .0182965    .0218838
           2     .0122801   .0009315    13.18   0.000    .0104186    .0141417
           3   (dropped)
  gender
           1     .0005275   .0009262     0.57   0.571   -.0013235    .0023784
           2   (dropped)
  major
           1    -.0028383   .0009783    -2.90   0.005   -.0047932   -.0008833
           2   (dropped)
  ----------------------------------------------------------------------------
```

ESTIMATING TREATMENT EFFECTIVENESS REDUCING DIMENSION 4: KNOWLEDGE OF THE LIBRARY ANXIETY RESULTS USING ANOVA – 2007 SURVEY, FULL SAMPLE

```
                    Number of obs =      71    R-squared     =  0.9767
                    Root MSE      = .003973    Adj R-squared =  0.9741

        Source |  Partial SS    df       MS              F     Prob > F
   ------------+----------------------------------------------------------
         Model |  .041734438     7  .005962063         377.67    0.0000
               |
         group |  .024259067     3  .008086356         512.23    0.0000
      libvisits |  .002304628    2  .001152314          72.99    0.0000
        gender |  .000076849     1  .000076849           4.87    0.0310
         major |  .000138184     1  .000138184           8.75    0.0043
               |
      Residual |  .000994547    63  .000015786
   ------------+----------------------------------------------------------
         Total |  .042728985    70  .000610414


        Source |     SS          df       MS            Number of obs =      71
   ------------+------------------------------           F(  8,    63) = 1064.52
         Model |  .134440306     8  .016805038          Prob > F      =  0.0000
      Residual |  .000994547    63  .000015786          R-squared     =  0.9927
   ------------+------------------------------           Adj R-squared =  0.9917
         Total |  .135434853    71  .001907533          Root MSE      =  .00397


   -----------------------------------------------------------------------------
       gain_D4       Coef.   Std. Err.      t    P>|t|     [95% Conf. Interval]
   -----------------------------------------------------------------------------
   group
             1    .0487929   .0013539    36.04   0.000    .0460874    .0514984
             2    .0569038   .0017806    31.96   0.000    .0533456     .060462
             3   -.0068224    .001583    -4.31   0.000   -.0099858   -.0036589
             4    .0300329   .0014307    20.99   0.000    .0271739     .032892
   libvisits
             1    .0141635   .0011803    12.00   0.000    .0118048    .0165222
             2    .0074915    .001225     6.12   0.000    .0050434    .0099395
             3   (dropped)
   gender
             1   -.0026874    .001218    -2.21   0.031   -.0051215   -.0002534
             2   (dropped)
   major
             1   -.0038061   .0012865    -2.96   0.004    -.006377   -.0012353
             2   (dropped)
   -----------------------------------------------------------------------------
```

ESTIMATING TREATMENT EFFECTIVENESS REDUCING
DIMENSION 5: MECHANICAL BARRIERS ANXIETY
RESULTS USING ANOVA – 2007 SURVEY, FULL SAMPLE

```
                     Number of obs =       71    R-squared     =  0.9935
                     Root MSE      = .009364    Adj R-squared =  0.9928

           Source |  Partial SS    df        MS              F      Prob > F
      -----------+----------------------------------------------------------
            Model |  .850259024     7  .121465575        1385.28     0.0000
                  |
            group |  .610721392     3  .203573797        2321.70     0.0000
         libvisits |  .000110663     2  .000055331           0.63     0.5354
           gender |  .001299826     1  .001299826          14.82     0.0003
            major |  .001290925     1  .001290925          14.72     0.0003
                  |
         Residual |  .005524045    63  .000087683
      -----------+----------------------------------------------------------
            Total |  .855783068    70  .012225472


        Source |       SS       df       MS              Number of obs =       71
   ------------+-----------------------------         F(  8,     63) =  1970.50
         Model |  1.3822379      8  .172779738         Prob > F       =   0.0000
      Residual |  .005524045    63  .000087683         R-squared      =   0.9960
   ------------+-----------------------------         Adj R-squared  =   0.9955
         Total |  1.38776195    71  .019545943         Root MSE       =   .00936


   -----------------------------------------------------------------------------
      gain_D5 |      Coef.   Std. Err.      t    P>|t|     [95% Conf. Interval]
   -----------------------------------------------------------------------------
   group       |
            1 |   .1196914   .0031908     37.51   0.000     .1133151    .1260677
            2 |  -.0860355   .0041964    -20.50   0.000    -.0944214   -.0776497
            3 |    .265359   .0037309     71.13   0.000     .2579035    .2728145
            4 |    .082674   .0033718     24.52   0.000     .0759359    .0894121
   libvisits   |
            1 |  -.0028062   .0027818     -1.01   0.317    -.0083652    .0027528
            2 |  -.0024771   .0028871     -0.86   0.394    -.0082465    .0032923
            3 |  (dropped)
   gender      |
            1 |  -.0110525   .0028706     -3.85   0.000     -.016789    -.005316
            2 |  (dropped)
   major       |
            1 |   .0116334   .0030319      3.84   0.000     .0055747    .0176922
            2 |  (dropped)
   -----------------------------------------------------------------------------
```

Appendix D: Demographics of Students Sampled

Table D.1. Survey Breakdown of Students Sampled by Number of Library Visits and Gender – 2006

| | libvisits and gender | | | | | | | | |
| | ---------0 to 2--------- | | | ---------3 to 5--------- | | | ------------>5------------ | | |
Group	Female	Male	Total	Female	Male	Total	Female	Male	Total
Online	1	5	6		1	1	2	5	7
Control	1	10	11	1	2	3	1	3	4
1-on-1	5	4	9	1		1	4	1	5
Group	2		2	5	1	6	13	4	17
Total	9	19	28	7	4	11	20	13	33

Table D.2. Survey Breakdown of Students Sampled by Major and Gender – 2006

| | major and gender | | | | | |
| | ---------Business--------- | | | ------Non-Business------ | | |
Group	Female	Male	Total	Female	Male	Total
Online	3	9	12		2	2
Control	2	7	9	1	8	9
1-on-1	4		4	6	5	11
Group	20	4	24		1	1
Total	29	20	49	7	16	23

Table D.3. Survey Breakdown of Students Sampled by Number of Library Visits and Gender – 2007

| | libvisits and gender | | | | | | | | |
| | ---------0 to 2--------- | | | ---------3 to 5--------- | | | ------------>5------------ | | |
Group	Female	Male	Total	Female	Male	Total	Female	Male	Total
Online	3	6	9	3	2	5		3	3
Control	3	3	6	2		2	3	4	7
1-on-1	3		3	3		3	7	1	8
Group	3	1	4	7	1	8	12	1	13
Total	12	10	22	15	3	18	22	9	31

Table D.4. Survey Breakdown of Students Sampled by Major and Gender – 2007

| | major and gender | | | | | |
| | ---------Business--------- | | | ------Non-Business------ | | |
Group	Female	Male	Total	Female	Male	Total
Online		3	3	6	8	14
Control	8	5	13		2	2
1-on-1	1		1	12	1	13
Group	4	2	6	18	1	19
Total	13	10	23	36	12	48

References

Alpert, Richard, and Ralph Norman Haber. 1960. Anxiety in academic achievement situations. *Journal of Abnormal and Social Psychology* 61, no. 2: 207-216.

Andrews, Judith. 1991. An exploration of students' library use problems. *Library Review* 40: 5-14.

Andrews, Bernice, and John M. Wilding. 2004. The relation of depression and anxiety to life-stress and achievement in students. *British Journal of Psychology* 95: 509-521.

Antell, Karen. 2004. Why do college students use public libraries? A phenomenological study. *Reference & Users Services Quarterly* 43, no. 3 (spring): 227-236.

Behr, Michele D., Maira Bundza, and Barbara J. Cockrell. 2007. Going for the gold: Recruiting students and engaging administrators through education and entertainment in the library. *College & Undergraduate Libraries* 14, no. 1: 1-18.

Biggs, Mary M. 1979. On my mind 'the perils of library instruction.' *Journal of Academic Librarianship* 5 (July): 159.

Bostick, Sharon L. 1992. The development and validation of the Library Anxiety Scale. Ph.D. diss., Wayne State University.

Cahoy, Ellysa Stern, and Rebecca Merritt Bichel. 2004. A luau in the library? A new model of library orientation. *College & Undergraduate Libraries* 11, no. 1: 49-57.

Clayton-Pedersen, Alma R., and O'Neill, Nancy. 2005. Curricula designed to meet 21st-century expectation. In *Educating the Net Generation*, edited by Diana G. Oblinger and James L. Oblinger. Boulder, Colo.: Educase.

Cornett, Claudia E. 1983. *What you should know about teaching and learning styles.* Bloomington, Ind.: Phi Delta Kappa Educational Foundation.

Davidson, Nancy M. 1983. Bull's-eye! Hitting targets for BI at Winthrop College. *Florida Libraries* 33 (September/October): 7-8.

Davis, Mary. 1999. Bowling Green designates librarian for freshmen. *College & Research Libraries News* 60, no. 11: 895-896.

Davy, John, Kerry Audin, Michael Barkham, and Caroline Joyner. 2000. Student well-being in a computing department. In *Proceedings of 5th annual SIGCSE/SIGCUE conference on innovation and technology in computer science education: ITiCSE.* London: Academic Press.

DeBard, Robert. 2004. Millennials coming to college. *New Directions for Student Services* 106: 33-45.

Felder, Richard M., and Eunice R. Henriques. 1995. Learning and teaching styles in foreign and second language education. *Foreign Language Annuals* 28 (Spring): 21-31.

Gale, Margaret. 2006. Reaching out: Library ambassadors. *Libraries:* 6-7.

Grant, Annie. 2002. Identifying students' concerns taking a whole institutional approach. In *Students' mental health needs: Problems and responses,* edited by Nicky Stanley and Jill Manthorpe. London: Jessica Kinsley.

Hartman, Joel, Patsy Moskal, and Chuck Dziuban. 2005. Preparing the academy of today for the learner of tomorrow. In *Educating the Net Generation,* edited by Diana G. Oblinger and James L. Oblinger. Boulder, Colo.: Educase.

Hesketh, Anthony J. 1999. Towards an economic sociology of the student financial experience of higher education. *Journal of Education Policy* 14: 385-410.

Higham, Krista, Cheryl Lutz, and Marjorie Warmkessel. 2007. Library-Fest: Helping new students feel comfortable with library resources, services, and staff. Presented at Share the CommonWEALTH, PASSHE Library Conference Sponsored by SSHELCO, 22 March at Harrisburg, Pennsylvania.

Holman, Lucy. 2000. A comparison of computer-assisted instruction and classroom bibliographic instruction. *Reference & User Services* 40, no. 1 (Fall): 53-60.

Hopkins, Frances L. 1981. User instruction in the college library: Origins, prospects, and a practical program. In *College Librarianship,* edited by W. Miller and D.S. Rockwood, 173-204. Metuchen, N.J.: Scarecrow Press.

Hopkins, Frances L. 1982. A century of bibliographic instruction: The historic claim to professional and academic legitimacy. *College & Research Libraries* 43 (May): 192-198.

How the new generation of well-wired multitaskers is changing campus culture. 2007. *Chronicle of Higher Education* 53, no. 18: B10-B15.

Howe, Neil, and William Stauss. 2000. *Millennials rising: The next great generation*. New York: Vintage Books.

Hunter, Mary Stuart, and James S. Gahagan, 2003. It takes a year. *About Campus* (September-October): 31-32.

Jiao, Qun G., Anthony J. Onwuegbuzie, and Art. A. Lichtenstein. 1996. Library anxiety: Characteristics of 'at-risk' college students. *LISR* 18: 151-163.

Jiao, Qun G., and Anthony J. Onwuegbuzie. 1997. Antecedents of library anxiety. *Library Quarterly* 67, no. 4: 372-389.

Jiao, Qun G., and Anthony J. Onwuegbuzie. 1999a. Self-perception and library anxiety: An empirical study. *Library Review* 48, no. 3: 140-147.

Jiao, Qun G., and Anthony J. Onwuegbuzie. 1999b. Identifying library anxiety through students' learning-modality preferences. *Library Quarterly* 69, no.2: 202-216.

Jiao, Qun G., and Anthony J. Onwuegbuzie. 1999c. Is library anxiety important? *Library Review* 48, no. 6: 278-282.

Jiao, Qun G. and Anthony J. Onwuegbuzie. 2002. Dimensions of library anxiety and social interdependence: Implications for library services. *Library Review* 51, no. 2: 71-78.

Jiao, Qun G., and Anthony J. Onwuegbuzie. 2004. The impact of information technology on library anxiety: The Role of computer attitudes. *Information Technology and Libraries* (December): 138-144.

Jones, Steve. 2002. *The Internet goes to college: How students are living in the future with today's technology*. Washington, D.C.: Pew Internet & American Life Project http://www.pewinternet.org/PPF/r/71/report_display.asp

Joseph, Miriam E. 1991. The cure for library anxiety – it may not be what you think. *Catholic Library World* 63: 111-114.

Kaminski, Karen, Pete Seel, and Kevin Cullen. 2003. Technology literate students? Results from a survey. *EDUCASE Quarterly* 26, no. 3: 34-40.

Keefer, Jane A. 1993. The hungry rats syndrome: Library anxiety, information literacy, and the academic reference process. *RQ*, 32: 333-339.

Kuhlthau, Carol C. 1988. Developing a model of the library search process: Cognitive and affective aspects. *RQ* 28: 232-242.

Kuhlthau, Carol C. 1991. Inside the search process: Information seeking from the user's perspective. *Journal of the American Society for Information Science* 42 (June): 361-371.

Lippincott, Joan K. 2005. Net generation students and libraries. In *Educating the Net* Generation, edited by Diana G. Oblinger and James L. Oblinger. Boulder, Colo.: Educase.

Long, J. Scott. 1997. *Regression models for categorical and limited dependent variables.* Thousand Oaks, Calif.: SAGE Publications.

Long, J. Scott, and Jeremy Freese. 2006. *Regression models for categorical dependent variables using Stata.* 2nd edition. College Station, Tex.: Stata Press.

Lorenzen, Michael. 1995. Remember the gin & tonic: using alcohol to teach Boolean searching. *Library Instruction Round Table (LIRT)* 17, no. 4: 10.

Lorenzen, Michael. 2001. A brief history of library information in the United States of America. *Illinois Libraries* 83, no. 2: 8-18.

McEuen, Sharon Fass. 2001. How fluent with information technology are our students? *EDUCAUSE Quarterly* 24, no. 4: 8-17.

Maddala, G.S. (1983). *Limited-dependent and qualitative variables in econometrics.* Cambridge: Cambridge University Press.

Martin, Carolyn A., and Bruce Tulgan. 2001. *Managing generation Y.* New Haven, Conn.: HRD Press.

Mech, Terrance F., and Charles Brooks. 1995. Library anxiety among college students: An Exploratory study. Paper presented at 7th National Conference of the Association of College and Research Libraries, 30 March - 2 April, at Pittsburgh, Pennsylvania.

Mech, Terrance F., and Charles Brooks. 1997. Anxiety and confidence in using a library by college freshmen and seniors. *Psychological Reports* 81: 929-930.

Mellon, Constance A. 1986. Library anxiety: A grounded theory and its development. *College & Research Libraries* 47 (March): 160-165.

Monk, Evelyn. 2004. Student mental health. Part 2: The main study and reflections of significant issues. *Counseling Psychology Quarterly.* 17: 33-43.

Oblinger, Diana G., and James L. Oblinger. 2005. Is it age or IT: First steps toward understanding the Net Generation. In *Educating the Net* Generation, edited by Diana G. Oblinger and James L. Oblinger. Boulder, Colo.: Educase.

Online Computer Library Center (OCLC). 2002. How academic librarians can influence students' web-based information choices. OCLC white paper on the information habits of college students. http://www5.oclc.org/downloads/community/informationhabits.pdf.

Onwuegbuzie, Anthony J., and Qun G. Jiao. 2000. I'll go to the library later: The Relationship between academic procrastination and library anxiety. *College & Research Libraries* 61, no.1 (January): 45-54.

Onwuegbuzie, Anthony J., and Qun G. Jiao. 2004. Information search performance and research achievement: An empirical test of the anxiety-expectation mediation model of library anxiety. *Journal of the American Society of Information Science & Technology* 55, no. 1 (January): 41-54.

Phillips, Beeman N. 1971. *Anxiety and school related interventions*. Albany: The University of the State of New York.

Prensky, Marc. 2001. Digital native, digital immigrants, Part II: Do they really think differently. *On the Horizon* 9, no. 6. http://www.marcprensky.com/writing/Prensky%20-%20Digital%20Natives,%20Digital%20Immigrants%20-%20Part2.pdf (accessed February 12, 2008).

Ramirez, Jennii L. 1994. Reference rover: The hesitant patron's best friend. *College & Research Libraries News* 6: 354-357.

Roberts, Ron, and John Golding. 1999. The effects of economic circumstances on British students' mental and physical health. *Journal of American College Health* 48: 103-109.

Roberts, Ron, and Christiane Zelenyanski. 2002. Degrees of debt. In *Students' mental health needs problems and responses,* edited by Nicky Stanley and Jill Manthorpe. London: Jessica Kinsley.

Salisbury, Alan B. 1971. An overview of CAI. *Educational Technology* 11 (October): 48-50.

Sax, Linda. J. 2003. Our incoming students: What are they like? *About Campus* 8, no.3: 15-20.

Schiller, Anita R. 1965. Reference service: Instruction or information. *Library Quarterly* 35 (January): 52-60.

Schneider, Barbara, and David Stevenson. 1999. *The Ambitious generation: America's teenagers, motivated but directionless.* New Haven, Conn.: Yale University Press.

Shapiro, Judith R. 2002. Keeping parents off campus. *The New York Times* (August 22, Late Edition – Final), Section A; Column 2: 23.

Shrigley, Roger. 1981. Reader education. *New Library World* 82 (March): 42-43.

Spielberger, Charles D. 1972. Anxiety as an emotional state. In *Anxiety: Current trends in theory and research,* edited by Charles D. Spielberger. Vol 1. New York: Academic Press.

Stewart-Brown, Sarah, Julie Evans, Jacoby Patterson, Sophie Peterson, Helen Boll, John Balding, and David Regis. 2000. The health of students in institutions of higher education: An important and neglected public health problem? *Journal of Public Health Medicine* 22, no. 4: 492-499.

Strauss, William, and Neil Howe. 1991. *Generations: The history of America's future, 1584 to 2069.* New York: Morrow.

Tidwell, Sandra L. 1994. Reducing library anxiety with a creative video and in-class discussion at Brigham Young University. *Research Strategies* 12: 187-190.

Tiefel, Virginia M. 1995. Library user education: Examining its past, projecting its future. *Library Trends* 44, no. 2 (Fall): 318-339.

Tucker, Patrick. 2006. Teaching the Millennial generation. *The Futurist* 40: 7.

Turkle, Sherry. 1995. *Life on the screen: Identity in the age of Internet.* New York: Touchstone.

Van Scoyoc, Anna M. 2003. Reducing library anxiety in first-year students. *Reference & User Services Quarterly* 42, no. 4: 329-341.

Walker, Billie E. 2006. Using humor in library instruction. *Reference Services Review* 34, no. 1: 117-128.

Westbrook, Lynn, and Sharon DeDecker. 1993. Supporting user needs and skills to minimize library anxiety: Considerations for academic libraries. *The Reference Librarian* 40: 43-51.

Wilson, Patrick. 1979. On the use of records of research. *Library Quarterly* 49, no 2: 127-145.

Zhang, Li, Erin M. Watson, and Laura Banfield. 2007. The efficacy of computer-assisted instruction versus face-to-face instruction in academic libraries: A systematic review. *Journal of Academic Librarianship* 33: 478-484.